This book was made possible by the following:

PETRO-CANADA ® Petro-Canada

S The Sheraton Centre

CP Air

Canon CAMERAS

Kodak Kodak Canada Inc.

NEW YORK NEW YORK FILM WORKS

LowePRO A DIVISION OF LOWE ALPINE SYSTEMS   **DAYMEN** PHOTO MARKETING LTD

 Apple Computer

C&L Coopers &Lybrand

TILDEN Tilden Rent-a-car Company

The Exhibition *A Day In the Life of Canada* has been made possible by a generous grant from American Express Canada Inc.

AMERICAN EXPRESS

Debra Streuber Schulke

Jack Corn

First published 1984
by Collins Publishers
100 Lesmill Road
Don Mills, Ontario
Canada
M3B 2T5

Canadian Cataloguing in
Publication Data
Main entry under title:

A Day in the Life of Canada

Issued also in French under title:

Une journée dans la vie du
Canada.

ISBN 0-00-217380-8

1. Canada - Description and
travel - 1981 - Views.
I. Smolan, Rick.
II. Cohen, David.

FC59.D39 1984
917.1′04646′0222
C84-099179-7
F1017.D39 1984

Project Directors
Rick Smolan and David Cohen

Art Director
Leslie Smolan

Cover Photography
Roger Ressmeyer

Printed in Japan
First printing September 1984

10 9 8 7 6 5 4 3 2

A Day in the Life of
Canada

Photographed by 100 of the world's
leading photojournalists on June 8, 1984

Collins Toronto

a day in the life of Canada

March 1, 1984

Dear Photographer,

I'm writing to invite you to work on a project that David Cohen,
Douglas Kirkland and I are in the process of organizing here in
Canada. I'm a freelance photographer and for the past ten years I've
been working on assignments around the world for many magazines
including Time, Newsweek, Fortune, and National Geographic.

This year Canada will be the focus of a great deal of attention. Not
only will there be a new Prime Minister, but both the Queen and the
Pope will be visiting Canada. Thousands of photographers will be
covering these events but they will be concentrating on these world
leaders. In the past photographers have produced beautiful books on
Canada but they have concentrated primarily on the country's
magnificent scenery. Where are the photographic books on the People
of Canada? We have a unique opportunity to show the day-to-day life
and infinite variety of the Canadian people to the rest of the world.

This is what we have in mind: We want to position one hundred of the
world's best photographers throughout Canada and give each
photographer the same 24-hour period to capture a typical Canadian day
on film. The result of this 24-hour shoot will be a hardcover book to
be titled "A Day in the Life of Canada" (DITLOCA for short).

On Friday June 8, 1984 you will be asked to photograph a specific
aspect of Canadian life. The aim of this project is not to make the
definitive statement about Canada. Nor is the intention to
concentrate on the rich, the famous or the powerful. Instead, you
will be asked to apply your photographic skills to something even more
challenging: to make extraordinary photographs of ordinary events.

We will be giving each of you a specific assignment, but you will also
have the freedom to shoot whatever you discover by accident on the
day--the assignment is just a starting point. All we ask is that you
make great pictures.

If all goes well, the project will produce a large format hardcover
book, a one-hour television documentary, a calendar featuring the best
photographs from the project and a travelling exhibit of photographic
prints.

Although this project has the personal support of the Prime Minister,
the Governor General, the Minister of Small Business and Tourism, plus
sponsorship by a number of private companies, it is not a public
relations exercise or a tourist promotion. Everyone supporting the
project understands that you are journalists and they will have no
editorial control over what you shoot or what ends up in the book.

DITLOCA will be an honest look at Canada, not just another book of pretty picture postcards.

By the same token there is no guarantee that every photographer will get a picture in the book. That depends on whether you have a good day on June 8th.

At the moment, the twenty of us on staff are frantically putting the last pieces in place to make sure everything goes smoothly when you and the other photographers arrive. If working with us on this crazy idea appeals to you, here are a few things you need to know and a few things we need from you very quickly:

1) Biography: Don't be modest. We need as much information about your photography career as possible--awards, exhibits, books published, major magazine stories, etc. We would also appreciate a good photo of you--in action if possible.

2) Film: Kodak Canada will supply you with 30 rolls of film (Kodachrome, Ektachrome or Tri-X). It would help us to know your requirements in advance.

3) Ground Transportation: If your assignment requires it, you will be provided with a rental car.

4) Insurance: Although we have liability insurance for everyone working on the project (e.g. if you drop your camera on the mayor's daughter's head, we are covered), we will not be able to insure you personally (e.g. if you get caught in an avalanche, you are not covered). You must have your own insurance.

5) Roommates: If you take advantage of the hotel rooms provided to you courtesy of the Sheraton Centre during your stay in Toronto, you will share a twin room with a famous photographer at absolutely no extra charge.

6) Payment: All expenses including air and ground travel will be covered by us. You will be paid an honorarium of $500 for the day's shooting.

We will be sending out more information to each photographer in the next few days but in the meantime, this letter is to ask if the idea interests you and if you will be able to join us. We hope you can make it.

Best regards,

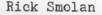

Rick Smolan

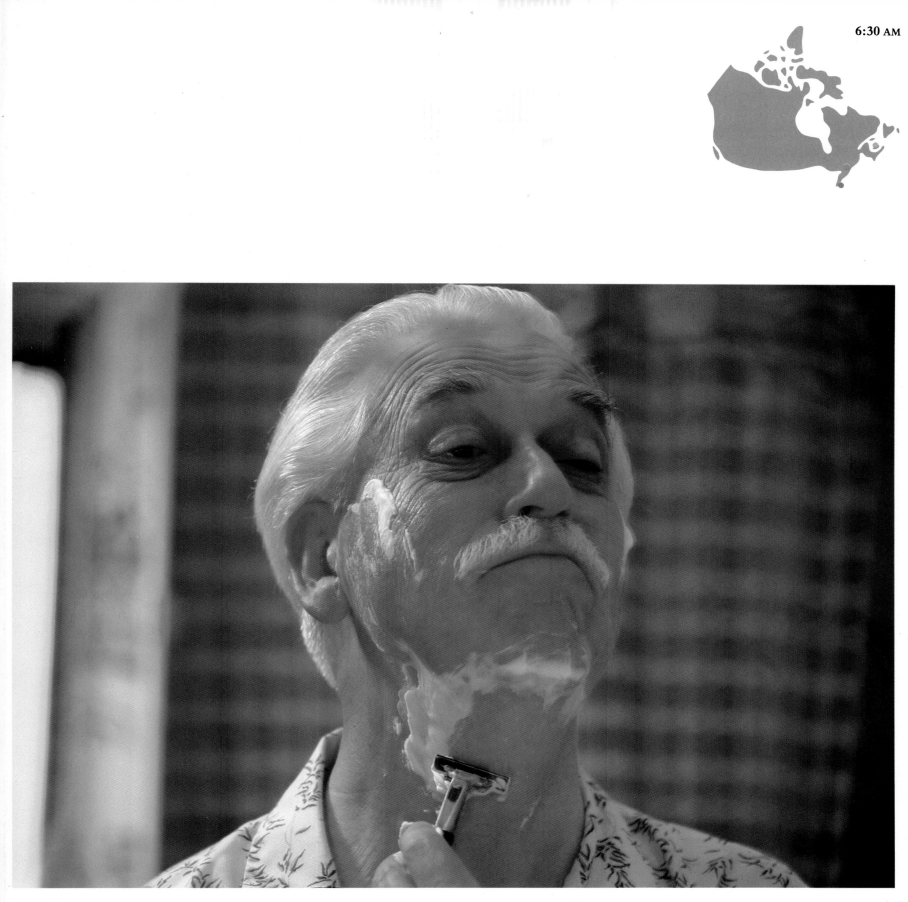

● *Previous page*

Lesley Boggs bugles campers awake at the Wilderness Tours campsite near the Ottawa River. John Whittle, anxious to tackle the river's famous white-water rapids, hears her song.

Photographer:

Gary Hershorn

● *Left*

A lonely farmhouse in the French River area of Prince Edward Island. Jacques Cartier landed on the coast of P.E.I. in 1534 and called it "the best tempered land one can possibly see."

Photographer:

Paul Chesley

● *Above*

Morley Kirkland of Fort Erie, Ontario shaves before a breakfast which will include a healthy slice of his wife Evelyn's famous rhubarb pie. The photo is by Hollywood glamor photographer, Douglas Kirkland, who has not watched his father shave since he was a small boy.

Photographer:

Douglas Kirkland

● *Previous page*

Shannon and Sarah Crosfield are getting ready for a day of high school.

New York photographer Andy Levin spent the morning of June 8th at the Crosfield home in Castlegar, British Columbia, a small city in the glorious west Kootenay country. Levin says, "When you work closely with a family and they trust you, you can freeze on film some of those small, intimate moments which make up the fabric of life. I don't consider this work. It's an opportunity to communicate the pleasure of life."

Photographer:

Andy Levin

● *Below*

At 7:00, Bill White, a financial advisor, irons his trousers before leaving for work at the Bank of Canada.

Photographer:

Donna Ferrato

● *Following page*

The "On On Tea Garden" in Vancouver's Chinatown.

Photographer:

Jay Maisel

● *Following pages 18-19*

Crystal Budzich, 7, and Teresa Bower, 8, run to catch the school bus in Chauvin, Alberta. Bus driver, Cameron Dallyn has been driving the 40-kilometre (23-mile) run for thirty years.

Photographer:

Lynn Johnson

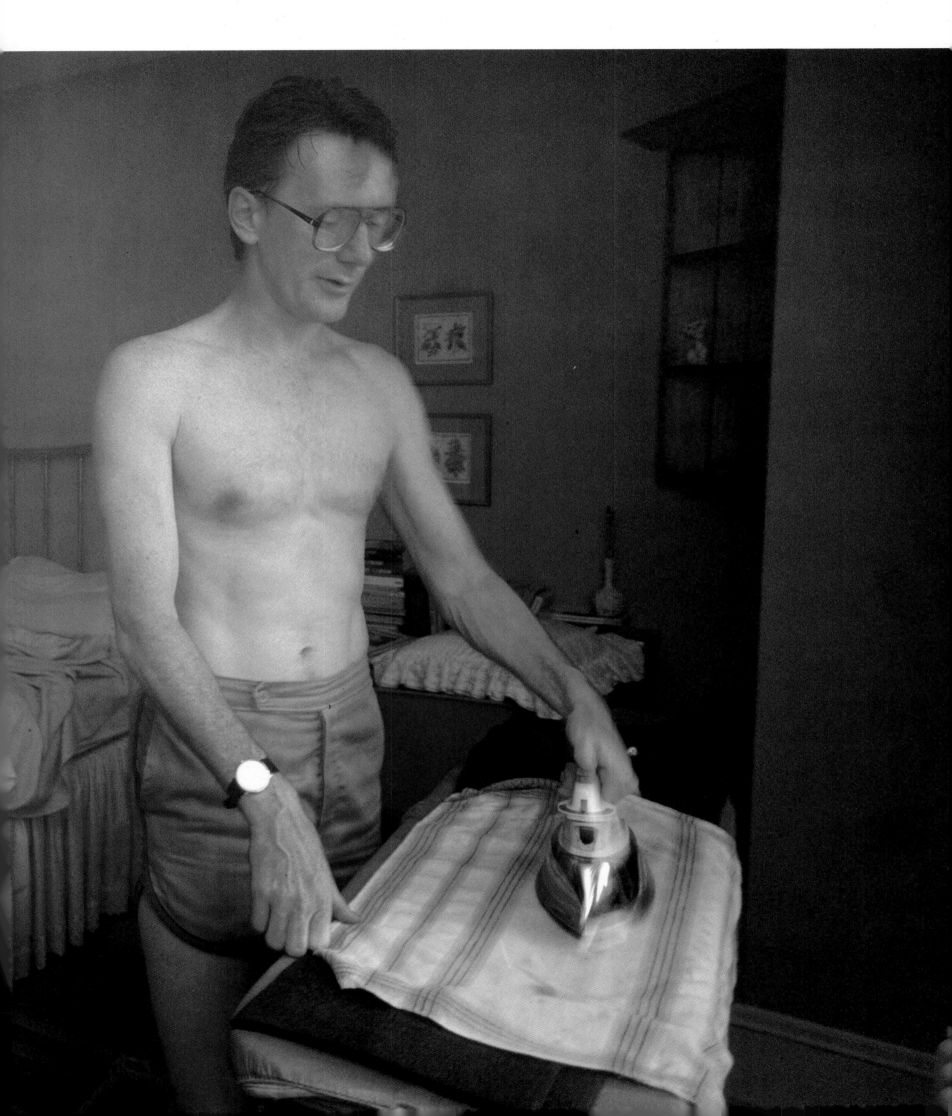

● *Previous page*

Ludwig and Renate Schmegelski lived in Russia, Yugoslavia and Austria before emigrating to Estevan, Saskatchewan in 1949. A retired car parker, Ludwig now fishes in a nearby lake. The postman arrives just as the Schmegelskis are about to cook the catch of the day.

Photographer:
Gerd Ludwig

● *Below,*

Despite other temptations, Lisa Gilvesy, 15, boards the school bus in London, Ontario at 8:15 AM.

Photographer:
Peter Martin

● *Below*

One hundred thousand of Manitoba's one million residents are of Ukrainian descent. The first-grade class at the Smith-Jackson School in Dauphin begins each morning in English, then speaks Ukrainian after lunch. Since it's morning, Ryan Campbell and Trish Harrison are exchanging secrets in English.

Photographer:
Hans Deryk

● *Right*

On her farm in Breadalbane, Prince Edward Island, Christine Stanley plays surrogate mother to these kids at feeding time.
Photographer:
Kent Kobersteen

● *Right*

Clarence Gauthier finds time to repair one of his 300 lobster traps. Gauthier grew up on Prince Edward Island and has been a lobster fisherman all his life.
Photographer:
Douglas Ball

● *Right*

In Estevan, Saskatchewan, William Hinzman, 71, shows granddaughter Christine, 2, where milk comes from.
Photographer:
Gerd Ludwig

An early morning stroller walks a breakwater in Victoria, with only Washington's Olympic Mountains for company.

Photographer:
Anthony Edgeworth

A Panarctic Oils crew "flares a well" on King Christian Island, 1,200 kilometres (750 miles) above the Arctic Circle. The procedure involves burning off the natural gas which accumulates in oil lines. Photographer Sam Garcia reports that the flare erupted with a noise which completely deafened him for two hours.

Photographer:
Sam Garcia

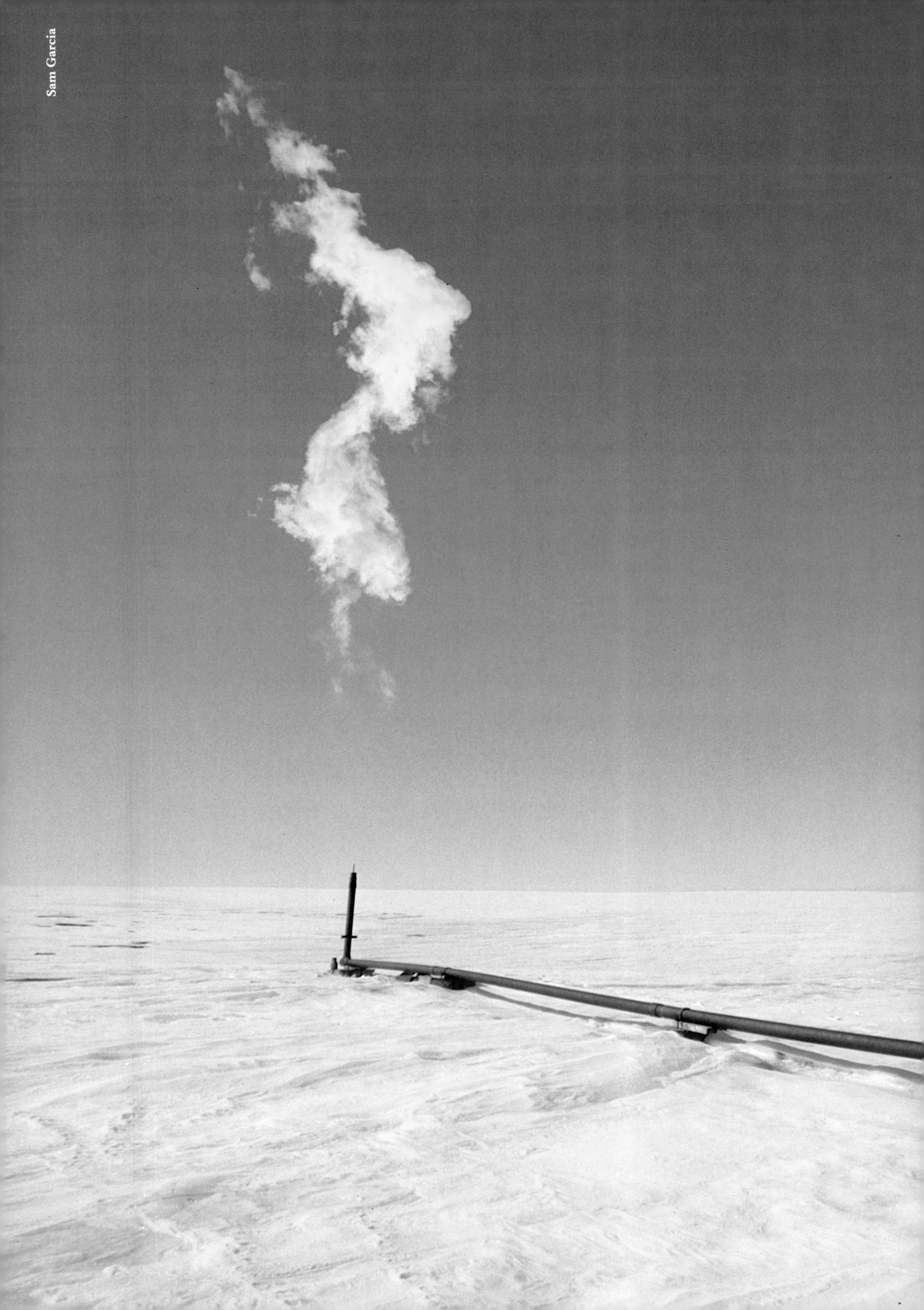

Sam Garcia

● *Left*

As an Inuit, Jeannie Keevik is
probably descended from
Asians who migrated across
the Bering Strait from Siberia
five millennia ago.

Photographer:
Harry Mattison

● *Above*

Bear Glacier, near Stewart,
British Columbia. Humorist
Stephen Leacock reflected that
"compared to the rest of the
troubled world, the North
seems like a vast realm of
peace."

Photographer:
Bill Frakes

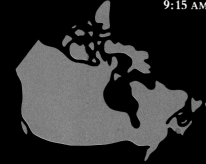

● *Left and above*

Photographer Freeman
Patterson spent June 8th
exploring his own backyard,
the Saint John River Valley.
The photographs on these
pages reaffirm his position
as one of Canada's most
respected nature
photographers.

● *Following page*

Retired schoolteacher Norma
Dykeman tends her green-
house in Fairvale, New Brunswick.

Photographer:
Freeman Patterson

The photographs on this page were all taken at exactly 9 AM. Each of the 100 photographers working on *A Day in the Life of Canada* had been asked to photograph a small business owner in front of his or her establishment.

Jay Maisel

Kim Stallknecht

BARBER

Ardenode, Alberta

Kent Kobersteen

Vancouver, British Columbia

Michael O'Brien

Toronto, Ontario

Winsloe, Prince Edward Island

Sturgeon, Prince Edward Island

Douglas Ball

Misha Erwitt

Winnipeg, Manitoba

Eric Hayes

Yellowknife, Northwest Territories

Calgary, Alberta

Bill Simpkins

● *Above*
Publisher W. Lawrence Heisey
and his wife Ann lean against
the Cadillac, while their
chauffeur, Thomas, uncovers
the Rolls. Mr. Heisey is chairman of the board of Harle-
quin Enterprises, Toronto,
the world's largest publisher
of romance novels.
Photographer:
Douglas Kirkland

● *Right*
Farmer John Worrell of
Ribstone gets his mail at the
Chauvin, Alberta post office.
Worrell inherited his farm
from his father who got it as a
"soldier's settlement" after
World War I. Many Alberta
veterans prospered when oil
was discovered on their land
in the late 1940s.
Photographer:
Lynn Johnson

● *Following page*
The Coast Mountains near
Prince Rupert, British Co-
lumbia.
Photographer:
Al Harvey

E ven before Confederation in 1867, Canada's lumber industry had been supplying the needs of the Industrial Revolution in Great Britain and the United States.

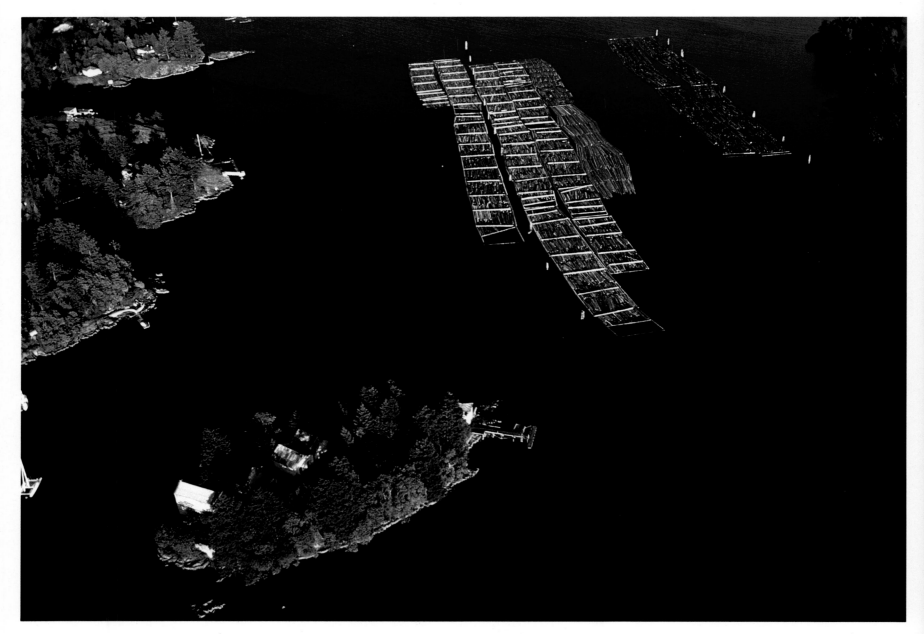

● *Above*

Log booms in Esquimalt harbor. About a quarter of the marketable timber in North America grows in the temperate coastal climate of British Columbia.

Photographer:
Anthony Edgeworth

● *Right*

Draune Nojonen, 22, inspects railroad cars in Thunder Bay, Ontario. Here he passes logs bound for a paper mill.

Over 275,000 Canadians make their living in the forestry industry. Annual production is valued in excess of four billion dollars, placing Canada's three million square kilometres (1.2 million square miles) of productive forest land among the country's most valuable natural resources.

Photographer:
Aaron Chang

Today, in British Columbia, lumber, pulp and paper, veneer and plywood are still produced from the province's magnificent forests. B.C. mills, alone, supply one-third of Canada's own pulp and paper needs and provide enough lumber each year to build at least a million houses.

Ontario and Quebec are also very important suppliers of pulp and paper and in the Atlantic Provinces, the traditional use of lumber for ship-building and barrel-making has been supplanted by today's requirements for newsprint and other paper products at home and abroad.

● *Far left*

Sawdust and scraps are burned off at the Westar lumber mill in Vanderhoof, British Columbia. Lumber is Vanderhoof's major industry. The Westar mill employs 200 men and women.

Photographer:

Grant Black

● *Left*

Harold Kipper is "tailing" the saw at Fraser's Lumber Products in White Falls, Ontario. The lumberyard employs twelve men and has been operating since 1939.

Photographer:

Marilyn Mikkelson

● *Above*

B.C. Forest Products Ltd. in Victoria.

Photographer:

Anthony Edgeworth

● *Following page*
Chinese fieldworkers tend vegetables on a farm near Vancouver. Although only three percent of British Columbia's population is of Chinese descent, Vancouver has the second largest Chinatown in North America
Photographer:
Jim Nachtwey

● *Left*

Engineer Ken Mason runs the "Royal Hudson," an authentic steam locomotive that travels between Vancouver and Squamish, British Columbia, taking summer visitors on daily sightseeing excursions. Sometimes, the coal-fuelled engine pulls five luxuriously appointed cars once used by HM Queen Elizabeth and her entourage to cross Canada. These can now be chartered by anyone wishing to view the snow-capped Rockies in particularly grand style.
Photographer:
Mike Shayegani

● *Above*

Jean Piché has worked at the Royal Canadian Mint for forty years, longer than any other employee. Piché pours molten gold into moulds before it solidifies. Here he demonstrates his steady hand to assistant Guy Gravel.
Photographer:
Gregory Heisler

● *Above, right*

Before they can be stamped, blank coins must be examined for imperfections. Marie Vallières, 58, inspects 200,000 one-cent coins during her daily eight-hour shift at the Royal Canadian Mint. In ten years at the mint, she's looked at approximately 480 million pennies. It costs 1.5 cents to produce a one-cent coin.
Photographer:
Gregory Heisler

Niagara Falls, which straddles the international border between Ontario and New York state actually consists of two falls. Goat Island splits the cataract into the American Falls and the more spectacular Horseshoe or Canadian Falls which, at 675 metres (2,200 feet), is more than twice as wide.

Formed 10,000 years ago by retreating glaciers, Niagara Falls provides hydroelectric power to both Canada and the United States. Its two border cities cater to tourists— particularly honeymooners—from nearly every country in the world. No one knows why Niagara Falls became the world's honeymoon capital.

One legend has it that Napoleon Bonaparte's brother set the trend when he made the long stagecoach trip to the falls after his wedding in New Orleans.

Picture Story by Dilip Mehta

● *Left*

Niagara Falls is still Canada's top tourist spot, attracting twelve to fourteen million visitors each year. For $5.95, at the Maple Leaf Shopping Centre, these would-be daredevils of yore can show their friends at home how they went over the falls in a barrel.

● *Top*

The changing room at Table Rock Scenic Tunnels. After donning their slickers, these visitors from Japan will brave heavy spray to view Niagara from points cut through the rock behind the falls.

● *Bottom and previous page*

For decades, the *Maid of the Mist* has carried tourists from around the world toward the thundering spectacle of Horseshoe Falls. The current vessel is actually *Maid of the Mist #4.*

● *Left*

Krista is on a day trip to Niagara Falls with her mother.

Photographer:

Dilip Mehta

● *Above, top*

Richard Benfield, left, is enjoying a snack in Edmonton's Churchill Square. His benchmate is the creation of sculptor J. Seward Johnson, Jr.

Photographer:

Tom Skudra

● *Above*

This figure in the window at Louis Tussaud's Waxworks in Niagara Falls has an air pump to simulate breathing.

Photographer:

Dilip Mehta

● *Below, top*

● *Below, top*

Less is more for sunbathers soaking up the June sun at Toronto's Sheraton Centre hotel.

Photographer:

Abbas

● *Below, middle*

Making the most of the sun in Toronto.

Photographer:

Abbas

● *Below, bottom*

Sun worshippers enjoy the day in Murdochville on Quebec's Gaspé Peninsula.

Photographer:

Micha Bar-am

● *Right*

"Sunbathing" in Dartmouth.

Photographer:

Lynn Goldsmith

● *Above*

Calgary's Kelly Kryczka, 22, has been "swimming synchro" since she was 8. She is one-half of the world championship synchronized swimming duet of Kryczka and Hambrook.

Photographer:
Dave Lazarowich

● *Right*

The Terry Fox Memorial stands beside the Trans-Canada Highway near Thunder Bay, Ontario.

Fox was 19 when his right leg was amputated because of bone cancer. Undaunted, Fox drew up a plan to run across Canada on one leg to raise funds for cancer research. On April 12, 1980, he began his "Marathon of Hope" in St. John's, Newfoundland. By September 1, 1980, he had run over 4,000 kilometres (2,500 miles).

On the site of this monument, Terry Fox was forced to give up his run. The cancer had spread to his lungs, and he was confined to hospital. Fox died ten months later, after raising more than twenty million dollars for cancer research and capturing the imagination of Canada and the world.

Day and night, travellers stop to view the statue on a stretch of road which has been renamed Courage Highway.

Photographer:
Aaron Chang

● *Left*

Ted Crosfield and Dolores
Aberdeen in their home in
Castlegar, British Columbia.
Ted lost his leg in an aviation
accident.
Photographer:
Andy Levin

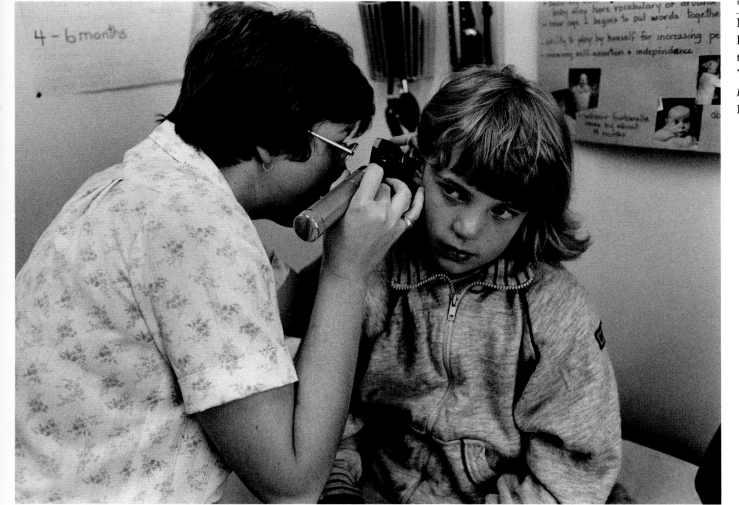

● *Left*

German-born Karen Empey,
37, clips poodles in her
Estevan, Saskatchewan home.
Business is good, and at
11:00 AM four poodles are
waiting for a trim.
Photographer:
Gerd Ludwig

● *Left*

Nurse Carol Thomas examines
Rea Postoloski at a health cen-
tre in Haines Junction,
Yukon Territory.
Photographer:
Bob Anderson

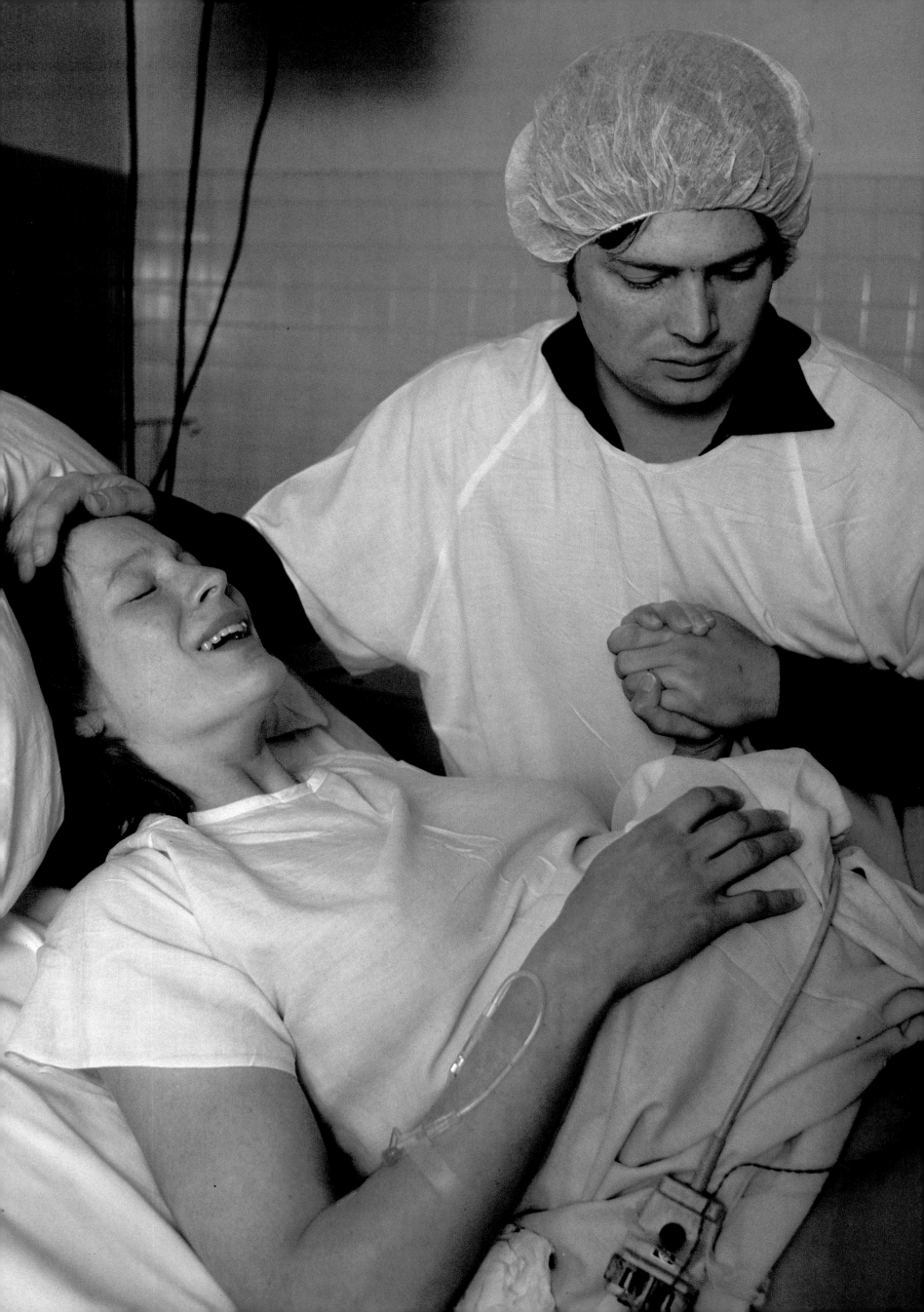

● *Left*

Thomas Clahane stands by as his wife, Deborah, prepares to deliver their first child at Grace Maternity Hospital in Halifax. On June 8th, 1,022 babies were born across Canada.
Photographer:
Lynn Goldsmith

● *Above*

B.J. Annis, owner of a gym used by Calgary's top professional wrestlers, presents his one-year-old son, Matthew. Annio says, ''Kids will change your life, but I love 'em anyhow.''
Photographer:
Gary Chapman

● *Left*

William David Scow, "Umbo" to his family, was the hereditary chief of the Kwicksutainenk people. Born October 15, 1902, in Gwayasdums, British Columbia, he was buried on June 8, 1984 in Alert Bay. Scow was eulogized as a progressive leader and devoted father.

Photographer:

Kazuyoshi Nomachi

● *Above*

Visiting the grain silos of Veikle Seeds Ltd., Pedigree Seed Growers at Cut Knife, Saskatchewan.

Photographer:

Lynn Johnson

Elmira, the oldest and largest Mennonite community in Canada, is 120 kilometres (75 miles) and a century from Toronto. The Mennonites emigrated to this area from Pennsylvania early in the 19th century. Since that time, the Canadian Mennonites have split into several branches while continuing to share certain fundamental beliefs. The Mennonites refuse to bear arms or take oaths of allegiance, and they reject the importance of worldly goods and concerns.

Toronto Star photographer Andrew Stawicki, who emigrated to Toronto from Poland and West Germany in 1982, wanted to spend June 8, 1984 in a gentler place and time. He carried a bolt of cotton cloth as a gift, and he brought his wife and two young children along to help make friends among the family-oriented Mennonites.

Picture Story by Andrew Stawicki

● *Left*

A Mennonite farmer drives across his farmland near Elmira, Ontario. Only recently, some of the younger Mennonites have purchased black automobiles.

Shirley Martin kneads dough
for a rhubarb pie. Unlike
many Mennonite farm fami-
lies, the Martins have electri-
cal appliances and running
water.

During school lunch break,
the boys and the girls eat their
home-made lunches separately.
Starting at age six, Mennonite
children walk barefoot to
class. On their fourteenth
birthday, they leave school to
work on the farm.

● *Right*
On Friday afternoon, the Martin family drove into Elmira to buy necessities. Later, photographer Stawicki and his family returned home to Mississauga on Highway 401 at 100 kilometres (60 miles) per hour.

● *Below*
Mr. and Mrs. Henry Metzjar traded in their plow horses for an International Harvester tractor.

● *Below, bottom*
Mary Martin's hair is brushed by her grandmother. Traditionally, three generations of a Mennonite family live in the same house.

● *Previous page*

Canadian glamor photographer Douglas Kirkland spent his noon hour at a fashion show in the Eaton Centre–a 302-store shopping mall covering three city blocks in the heart of style-conscious Toronto.

Canadian designers are becoming increasingly important to the international fashion scene; the dresses shown here reflect the innovative style of Canadian, Tom D'Auria.

Photographer:

Douglas Kirkland

● *Below*

At the Rivoli restaurant on Toronto's bohemian Queen Street West, waitress Jennifer Snowsill gets a kiss over the condiments from John Paisley.

Photographer:

Jill Krementz

● *Below, top*
Trendy young browsers at the Eaton Centre, Toronto's downtown shopping mall, showplace, tourist attraction and gathering spot since 1977.
Photographer:
Abbas

● *Below, middle*
Lesley Saunders of Markham, Ontario and Gilles Fumat of Banff, Alberta enjoy a snowy day in Sunshine Village. June 8th is closing day at this popular ski resort in Alberta's Banff National Park.
Photographer:
Audrey Topping

● *Below, bottom*
Gossip on Toronto's Bloor Street.
Photographer:
Nicole Bengiveno

Photographer:
Susan Kivi

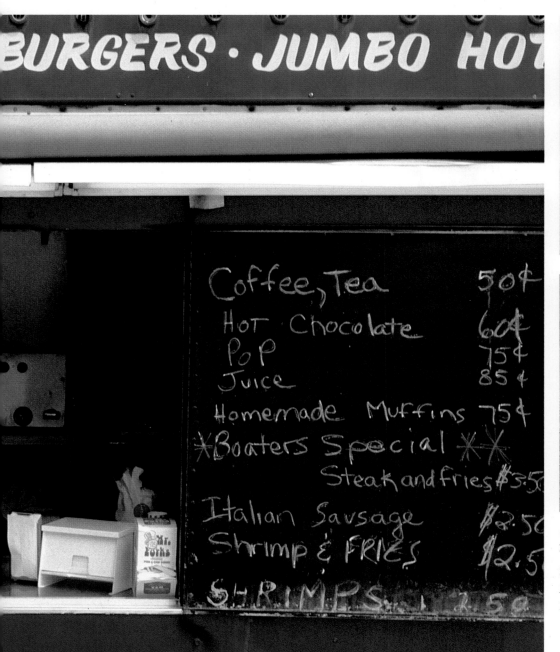

BURGERS · JUMBO HOT

Coffee, Tea   50¢
Hot Chocolate   60¢
Pop   75¢
Juice   85¢
Homemade Muffins 75¢
*Boaters Special **
           Steak and fries $3.50
Italian Sausage $2.50
Shrimp & FRIES $2.5

SHRIMPS 1750

ndwiches ✷ dogs

● *Above, top*

Two young gourmands in
Stanley Park, Vancouver.
Photographer:
Mike Shayegani

● *Above*

Lunchtime at the Granby
(Quebec) Zoo. Michel Jutras
feeds Patriarche, the zoo's full-
grown male hippopotamus.
Photographer:
Malak

● *Left*

A quick lunch, Toronto style.
Photographer:
Susan Kivi

● *Left*

A mobile home camp near Fort McMurray, Alberta.
Photographer:
Alon Reininger

● *Above*

The hundred-year-old Block House in Lunenburg County, Nova Scotia belongs to Daisy Ernst who moved to a smaller house across the street when the big house became "too much to handle." Mrs. Ernst's dog, Reba, still visits.
Photographer:
Lynn Goldsmith

● *Following page*

A flock of Canadian Forces "Snowbirds" soar over the Red River in Winnipeg, Manitoba. The Canadian aerial acrobatic team, which consists of nine two-man Tutor jets, is en route to the annual air show in Gimli, Manitoba.
Photographer:
Rick Smolan

A 500 tonne digging machine, called a dragline, dredges oil sands at the Syncrude surface mine near Fort McMurray, Alberta. One "cup" or shovelful holds enough oil sands to fill a normal one-car garage. The dragline dumps the petroleum rich mixture onto a conveyor belt which carries it to the refinery. The Syncrude project utilizes four draglines, each with a boom longer than a football field, to mine one of the richest oil-sand deposits in the world. The deposits were first discovered by Alberta's pioneers who used the oil to grease their wagon wheels.

Photographer:
Alon Reininger

12:22 PM: Gilbert Gagné, Lucien Boulanger and Ferdinando Cocchetto work at the Ogilvy flour mill in Montreal.

Photographer:
J. Carl Ganter

● *Left*

Some of the largest digging machines in the world operate in the coal pits of south Saskatchewan.

Photographer:
Gerd Ludwig

This RCAF Vulcan is now a monument in a small park in Goose Bay, Labrador.

Photographer:
Ken Kerr

The Château Frontenac, built between 1893 and 1895, was named for Louis de Buade, comte de Frontenac. Frontenac was a French aristocrat, courtier and soldier who served as governor of New France from 1672 until 1701. Still Quebec City's best-known hotel, the Château Frontenac has 492 rooms and is owned and operated by Canadian Pacific Hotels.

Photographer:
Frank Fournier

Sudbury, in Northern Ontario, is the nickel capital of North America. After spending the morning deep in the mines, photographer Alan Carruthers captured this silhouette on his way back to the surface.

Photographer:
Alan Carruthers

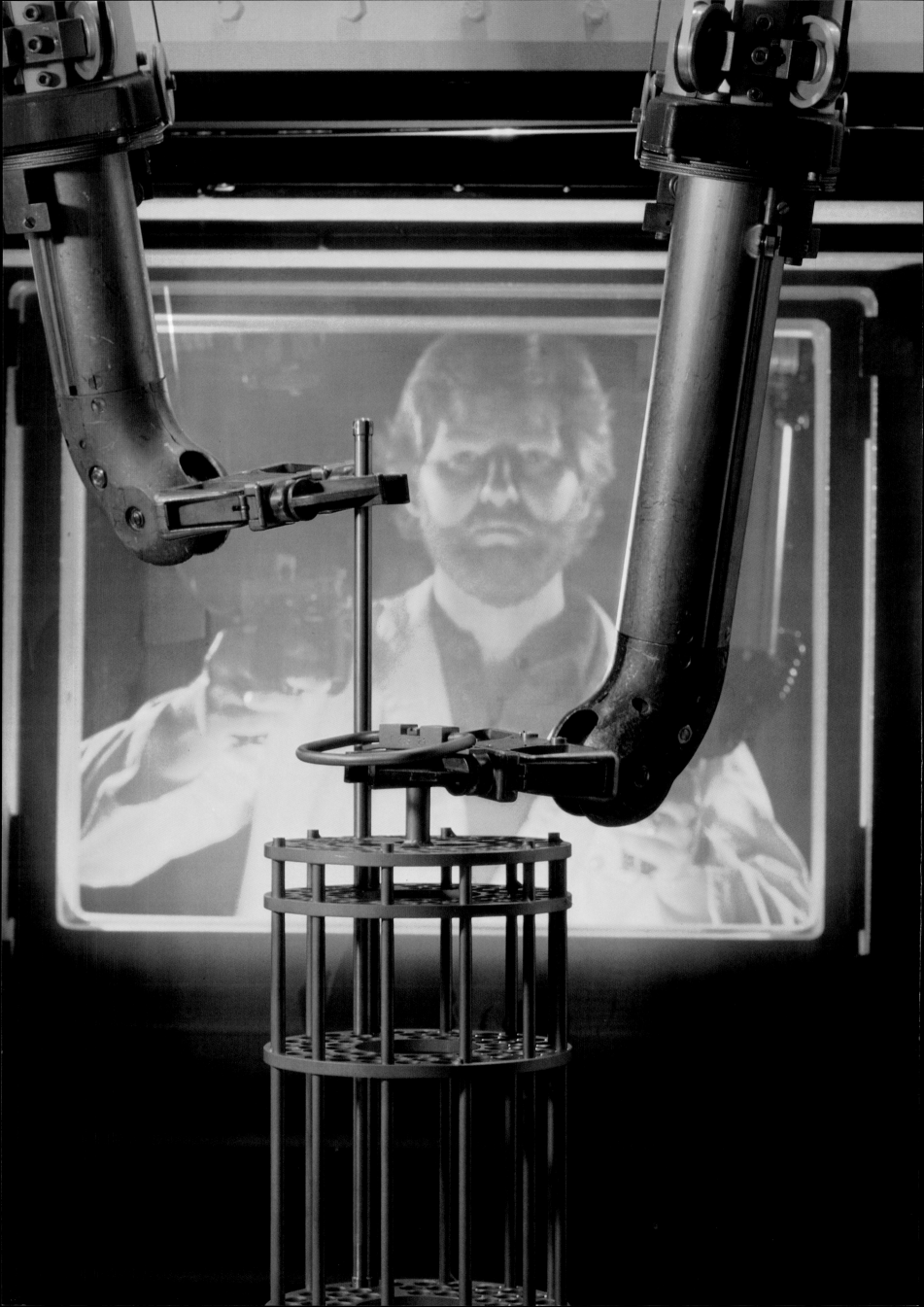

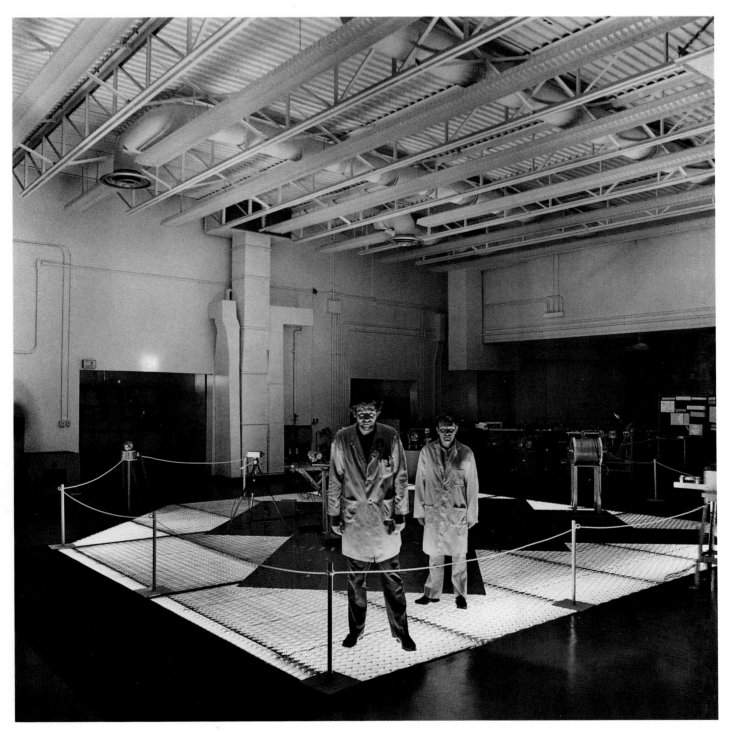

● *Left*

At the Atomic Energy of Canada (AEC) complex in Kanata, Ontario, technician Don Vean peers through a lead glass window. Vean uses a remote manipulator arm to load an irradiator pencil containing active cobalt-60 into a shipping cage. The shipping cage is then loaded into a shielded container for delivery.

AEC produces over half the radioactive diagnostic material used by doctors around the world. After making this picture from a shielded position inside the "hot cell," photographer Roger Ressmeyer and his equipment were scanned for radioactivity by plant security.

Photographer:

Roger Ressmeyer

● *Above*

Nuclear physicists Dave Rogers (left) and Len Van Zwan in the underground "target room" of a nuclear accelerator facility at the National Research Council in Ottawa.

Photographer:

Gregory Heisler

Anyone who likes shellfish would love Caraquet. This town in New Brunswick produces 19,000 tonnes of crab and lobster products each year. Caraquet's fishing boats, many of which are equipped with their own boiling and freezing facilities, tend wooden traps in the cold waters of Chaleur Bay.

The boats carry their catch back to packaging plants in Caraquet where the shellfish are steamed, shucked, cleaned and packaged.

A behind-the-scenes glimpse at Caraquet's Products Belle Baie and Bay Chaleur plants, which employ 700

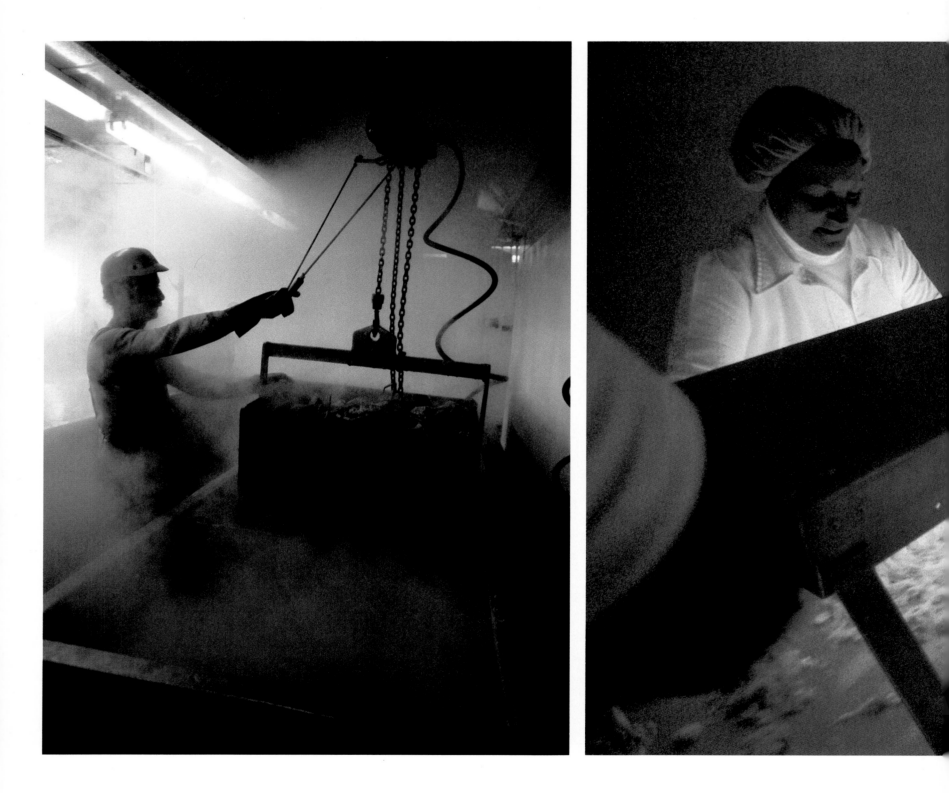

and 180 people, respectively, didn't seem to put Washington, D.C.-based photographer Stephanie Maze off her favorite delicacy. Maze says, "I had lobster in every shape and every form, morning, afternoon and night. I had broiled lobster, boiled lobster, fried lobster, lobster salad and lobster omelets. I think I'm going to miss that lobster for the rest of my life, the best lobster I ever tasted."

Picture Story by Stephanie Maze

● *Previous page*
At the Bay Chaleur packers plant, women known as "casseuses" or "shuckers" get every last bit of meat out of a crab leg by hook or by crook.

● *Above, left*
Crabs are steamed by the bucketful at the Bay Chaleur plant.

● *Above*
Workers at the Products Belle Baie plant "read" crabmeat under ultra-violet light which reveals any tiny shell or cartilage fragments that might be clinging to the meat.

● *Above, top*
Just off the boat, lobsters get a freshwater bath at the Products Belle Baie processing plant.

● *Above*
Ten thousand crabmeat cocktails are shovelled into a storage room at the Belle Baie processing plant.

● *Left*

During the refining process, a steelworker uses a long wooden rod to skim slag which has risen to the surface of the kettles. Canada has some of the largest iron ore reserves in the world and exports about two billion dollars' worth of iron and steel products each year.

Photographer:
Bill DeKay

● *Above*

Algoma slag skimmers face heat rising from the 1,600° C. (2,900° F.), steel baths.

Photographer
Bill DeKay

● *Left*

Because of its location near vast iron reserves and lake transportation, Sault Ste Marie, Ontario has steel as its main industry. Algoma Steel, where these photographs were taken, is one of Canada's largest manufacturers. The Algoma mill operates twenty-four hours a day, seven days a week, making the iron ore from its own mines into steel products which include plate, sheet, strip, seamless tubular and structural steel.

Photographer:
Bill DeKay

The volunteer fire department tug-of-war is a highlight of the annual Farmers Day Picnic in Ferintosh, Alberta (pop. 150). On June 8th, the winning team, from nearby Bashaw, defeated Edberg, New Norway and host team Ferintosh.

Photographer:
Petr Honcu

● *Left*

At the Canadian Forces
Base in Petawawa, Ontario,
officers of the Royal Canadian
Mounted Police engage in a
crowd control exercise. A
mob of "rioters" played by
soldiers from the base attacks a
mock parliament building,
chanting "We want beer"
and hurling tennis balls. The
building is defended by
RCMP officers wielding billy
sticks and smoke canisters.
According to photographer
Greg Stott, "Over the course
of two or three hours, on a
very hot and humid day, the
exercise got a little feisty.
Tempers flared, and billy sticks
were used with some force.
On the last pass, the RCMP,
against the orders of the
military, used real tear gas."
Photographer:
Greg Stott

● *Above*

Private Darryl Sutherland,
who played the part of an
agitator during the RCMP
crowd control exercise, was
caught by an unexpected
whiff of tear gas.
Photographer:
Greg Stott

Lunchtime at Warkworth
Medium Security Prison near
Peterborough, Ontario.
Warkworth houses men serv-
ing sentences from two to
twenty-five years.
Photographer:
Michel Gravel

● *Left*

Officer Douglas Kwiatkowski
checks holding cells at the
Royal Canadian Mounted Po-
lice headquarters in Dawson,
Yukon Territory.
Photographer:
Jay Dickman

● *Above*

Solitary confinement at
Warkworth Medium Security
Prison. On June 8th, there
were 26,924 inmates in Can-
ada's 445 prisons and jails.
Photographer:
Michel Gravel

● *Above*

The pool of the Dyconia
Hotel in Wasaga Beach,
Ontario.

Photographer:
Victor Fisher

● *Right*

Much of downtown Toronto
is linked by underground
concourses which are located
beneath major office com-
plexes and lined with popular
shops and restaurants. During the long winter months,
much of the life downtown
can be lived underground.

Photographer:
Abbas

Michael O'Brien

Nicole Bengiveno

Vince Streano

Al Harvey

Jim Wiley

MERCI - REVENEZ

Above

Yousuf Karsh, known as Karsh of Ottawa, is probably the world's most famous portrait photographer. Adam Jahiel caught up with Karsh, who spent June 8th working on a corporate job in Los Angeles, California.

Photographer:
Adam Jahiel

● *Right*

Life magazine picture editor John Loengard, a longtime admirer, visited Karsh's studio at Ottawa's Château Laurier Hotel. There he found Karsh's printer, Ignas Gabalis, who has worked with Karsh for over thirty years.

Loengard asked Gabalis to identify the photographer's most famous picture. Gabalis thought for a moment, put on a pair of white cotton gloves, opened the vault and pulled out this negative—Karsh's definitive portrait of Winston Churchill taken in 1941.

Photographer:
John Loengard

● *Left*
Reverend Iftemy Trufyn of St. George's Ukrainian Orthodox Church in Dauphin, Manitoba. The fifth largest ethnic group in Canada, many Ukrainians emigrated to the Prairies—which closely resemble the steppes of their homeland—in the early part of the twentieth century.
Photographer:
Hans Deryk

● *Above*
Before eating his lunch at La Trappe monastery, Oka, near Montreal, Brother Hilary, who is hard of hearing, listens to his abbot's blessing.

Brother Hilary belongs to the Cistercians, a Roman Catholic order founded in 1098. The Cistercians became known as the "White Monks" when they adopted white instead of the black of the Benedictines. The monastery sells Oka cheese which is well known throughout North America.
Photographer:
Roland Neveu

● *Following page*
Schoolyard, Lunenburg Academy.
Photographer:
Lynn Goldsmith

● *Following page 107*
It is not always easy to dry clothes on Grand Manan Island in New Brunswick.
Photographer:
Gail Harvey

● *Above, top*

Babysitter Terry Lyall shares
a joke with seven-month-old
Richard Tuttauk in Happy
Valley, Labrador.
Photographer:
Ken Kerr

● *Above*

Instructor Julie Dawley and
eighteen-month-old Chadwick
Lofthouse at the Moms and
Tots swimming class held at
the Tillsonburg (Ontario)
Community Centre.
Photographer:
Peter Martin

● *Right*

Six-year-old Sigrid Stefanson
visits her great-grandmother,
Gudney, at a retirement home
in Gimli, Manitoba. Gimli,
which means ''home of the
Gods'' in Icelandic, is a fishing community, half Icelandic
and half Ukrainian, on the
shores of Lake Winnipeg.
Photographer:
Maddy Miller

● *Above*

Despite the sign, these White-horse, Yukon taxidermists specialize in bearskin rugs. In a good year, Timberline skins about 200 bears.

Photographer:
Tedd Church

● *Right*

The Hotel Royale in Schefferville, Quebec is a family business. Lina Tortier, the assistant manager, works for her father, the proprietor.

Photographer:
Diego Goldberg

● *Right*

Cécile Chenard poses beneath the buck and moose antlers which are mounted on the outside wall of her home in Caraquet, New Brunswick.

Photographer:
Stephanie Maze

● *Following pages 112-113*

Pomp and circumstance: The graduating kindergarten class of St. Anthony's Elementary School, St. Anthony, Newfoundland.

Photographer:
Ottmar Bierwagen

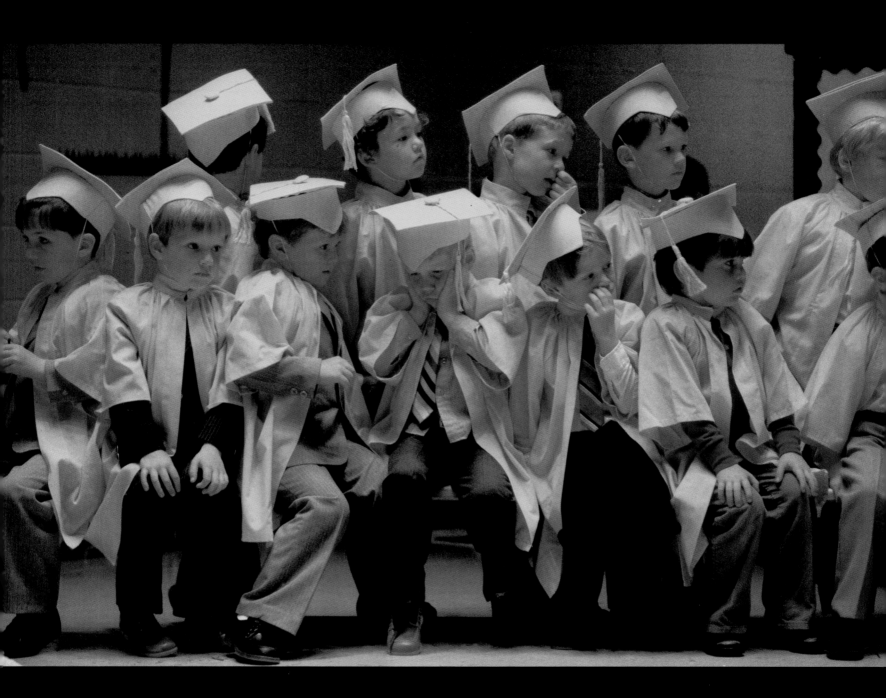

113

Ken Kerr

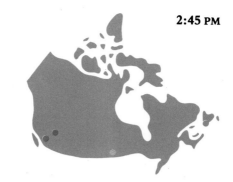

● *Previous page*

Built during World War II, Ernest Harmon Air Force Base in Stephenville, Newfoundland was abandoned to the dandelions by the U.S. Air Force in 1968.

Photographer:
Ken Kerr

● *Left*

Hikers on old country road to Pridding, Alberta. Canada's road system covers vast distances. The Trans-Canada Highway, the longest paved highway in the world, winds 7,500 kilometres (4,700) miles from St. John's, Newfoundland to Victoria, British Columbia.

Photographer:
Tom Walker

● *Above*

Ned Rathburn is a part-owner of the Headwaters Fishing Camp. The camp, which consists of six cabins with potbelly stoves, is located 1,300 metres (4,300 feet) high in British Columbia's Okanagan Mountains. Photographer Shelly Katz says, "On a cold mountain morning, running water means you grab a bucket, run down to the lake and run back."

Photographer:
Shelly Katz

● *Following page*

Alberta.
Photographer:
Lynn Johnson

● *Following page 119*

Saskatchewan.
Photographer:
Gerd Ludwig

● *Above*

Double vision in Sault Ste Marie's Bellevue Park. Stacy is on the left, Sheena on the right.

Photographer:
Bill DeKay

● *Right*

"I think I made a picture in a town south of Ottawa. A little girl named Angela was getting ready to go to her first communion. She was wearing a beautiful white dress, almost like a wedding gown. She was so cute, such a doll. Her brother, Trevor, was about to go play in a baseball game, but I asked them if I could take their picture. Trevor handed Angela his baseball bat so that he could get the family cat, Dot, into the picture. There was something intimate about the picture."

Photographer:
Roger Ressmeyer

children with disc cameras. In return for working on *A Day in the Life of Canada*, the children were allowed to keep their cameras. On this page is a selection of the 2,400 photographs shot by this army of young photographers.

Photographer: Fatima Machado, age 11

Photographer: Le Hoang Khanh, age 11

Photographer: Rory Cullen, age 10

Photographer: Susy Pedro, age 11

Photographer: Sophie Cyr, age 11

Photographer: Dina Mota, age 13

Photographer: Mark Moniz, age 7

Photographer: Sophie Cyr, age 11

Photographer: Thokoza Miller, age 10

Photographer: Le Hoang Khanh, age 11

Photographer: Cindy Ann Goulart, age 7

Photographer: Ryan White, age 12

● *Previous pages 124-125*
The Terminal City lawn
bowling team, champions of
British Columbia, are prac-
tising for the Canadian Na-
tional Championships which
will be held in Hamilton,
Ontario in August.
Photographer:
Ethan Hoffman

● *Previous page*
Faces waiting for bodies at the
Morgese Soriano mannequin
factory.
Photographer:
Michael O'Brien

● *Below*
The Morgese Soriano mannequin factory produces 1,500 to
2,000 complete body manne-
quins a year. Designers tailor
face and body styles according
to the dictates of fashion, gen-
erally set forth by the ladies'
wear sections of large department stores. The Toronto factory was founded in 1932 by
owner Nick Soriano's father.
Photographer:
Michael O'Brien

● *Following page*
Intrepid weekend oarsmen
negotiate Garvin's Shoot, the
most treacherous set of rapids
on the Ottawa River.
Photographer:
Gary Hershorn

Lynn Johnson

● *Previous pages 132-133*
On a wet spring afternoon, Jennifer and Kimberley Perry cross a wheatfield in the heart of Canada's breadbasket. The girls are visiting their grandfather's farm in Chauvin, Alberta. Alberta produces one-third of the grain exported by Canada each year.

Photographer:

Lynn Johnson

● *Previous page*
Goslings, communally owned by the Hutterite religious colony of Pincher Creek, Alberta, just before the afternoon feed.

Photographer:

P.F. Bentley

● *Below*

Sixteen volunteer cowhands have gathered at the Lazy J Ranch to help owner Alvin Kumlin with the branding. On June 8th they branded, ear marked and inoculated 280 calves. Afterwards they celebrated with steak, muffins and beer. The Kumlins have owned the 2,000 hectare (5,000 acre) Lazy J for four generations. "It was a surprise," said photographer Ken Heyman, "to find out that branding was a very festive occasion, a cultural tradition like a rite of spring."

Photographer:

Ken Heyman

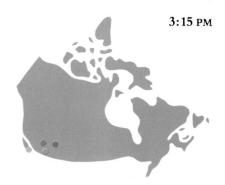

● *Above, top*

These cowboys from Warner and MacKenzie Guiding and Outfitting, Ltd. take tourists on trail rides through the Rockies in Banff National Park. Left to right are Ed Shubert, Yves Le Blanc, Dave Wright, Art DeBruin and Cyril Amy.

Photographer:
Robin Moyer

● *Above*

Harry ''Cougar'' Brown says he is 99 years old, but his neighbors in Port Alberni, British Columbia say he is only 93. Harry's dog, age unknown, is named Spot.

Photographer:
Arnaud de Wildenberg

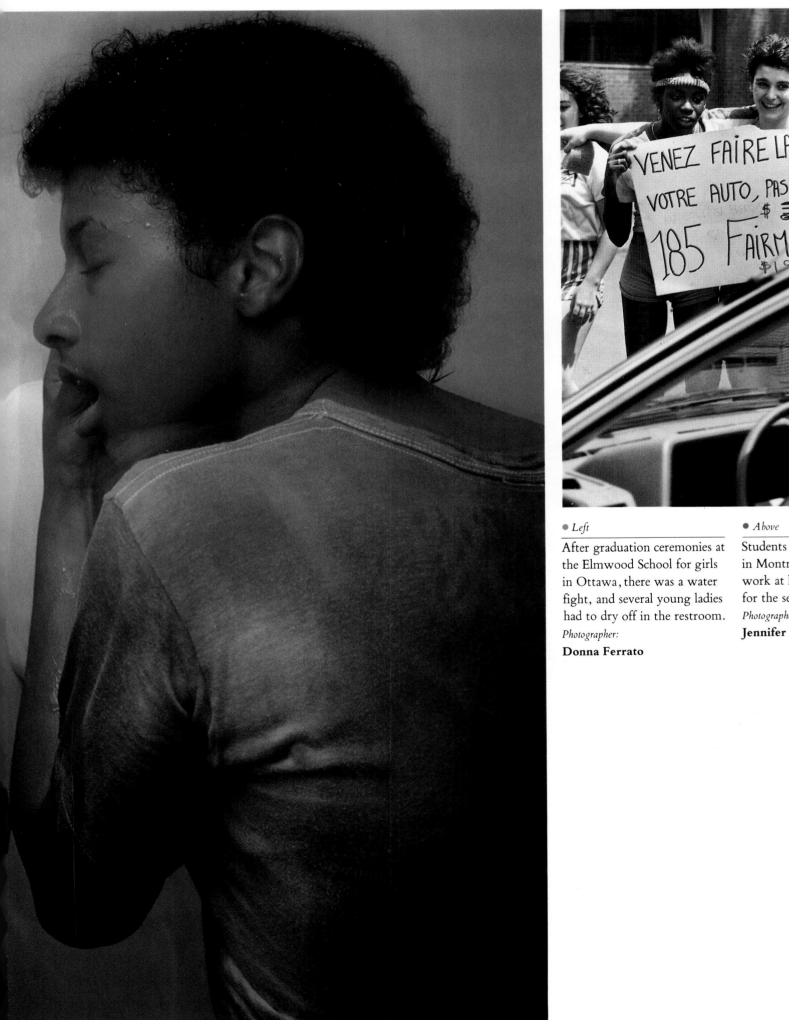

● *Left*

After graduation ceremonies at the Elmwood School for girls in Ottawa, there was a water fight, and several young ladies had to dry off in the restroom.
Photographer:
Donna Ferrato

● *Above*

Students at le Collège français in Montreal resort to hard work at low rates to raise cash for the senior prom.
Photographer:
Jennifer Erwitt

● *Above*

Mildred Hall Elementary
School in Yellowknife, North-
west Territories.
Photographer:
Eric Hayes

● *Right*

Old World Toronto.
Photographer:
Michael O'Brien

Spit and polish: A sergeant major barks orders to the Royal Canadian Regiment which is rehearsing for parade inspection at the Canadian Forces Base in Petawawa, Ontario.

Photographer:
Greg Stott

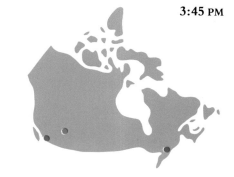

● *Above, top*

Navy League cadet Harlan Simpkins of Calgary is supposed to be practising his trumpet.

Photographer:
Gary Chapman

● *Above*

A call for action on the floor of the Vancouver Stock Exchange.

Photographer:
Ethan Hoffman

In the small town of Schefferville in northeastern Quebec, photographer Diego Goldberg of Argentina encountered an unexpected event. Goldberg had been scheduled to spend June 8th with Dominique Ashini, one of the great hunters of the Montagnais reserve. Instead, he found that Ashini, 50, had been killed during a caribou hunt.

● *Left and above*
Mourners surround the coffin of hunter Dominique Ashini outside the school gymnasium in Schefferville, Quebec.

● *Above, top*
Ashini's funeral mass was attended by most of Schefferville's citizens. The hunter's handmade canoe served as an altar.

Most of Schefferville's 1,300 townspeople attended Ashini's funeral in the school gymnasium. The hunter's handmade canoe served as the altar, and his children were pallbearers. The coffin containing Ashini's body was placed in a vault until later in the month when the earth would thaw, and a grave could be dug.

Picture Story by Diego Goldberg

● *Left*

At the Ashini home, family and friends share a meal of caribou. Ashini's father says the prayer.

● *Top*

Meanwhile, in an adjoining room relatives look at photographs of the late hunter.

● *Bottom*

Friends leave on the weekly train to Sept-Iles, nearly 400 kilometres (250 miles) to the south.

● *Previous page*

On June 8th, some of Canada's most spectacular scenery was shrouded in dense fog. Late in the afternoon, the mists parted long enough for Robin Moyer to get this glimpse of Cirrus Mountain in Banff, Canada's first and best known national park. Set in the heart of the Rockies, Banff was founded in 1885.

Photographer:
Robin Moyer

● *Left*

These dancers live at the National Ballet School in Toronto where they take academic, as well as dance classes. During a quiet moment between rehearsals, Canada's future ballerinas sign yearbooks.

Photographer:
Jill Krementz

● *Left*

Can-can dancers at Diamond-Tooth Gertie's, a gambling and dance hall in Dawson, Yukon Territory. Dawson was a boom town during the fabled Klondike gold rush of 1897-98.

Photographer:
Jay Dickman

● *Left*

Three-year-old prima ballerinas dance *The Enchanted Slipper* at the St. John's Arts and Culture Centre.

Photographer:
Boris Spremo

● *Below*

Luci Pettigrew's amateur hockey team in Quebec City. Ice hockey originated in Canada in the 1870s and has since become a national passion.
Photographer:
Jean-Pierre Laffont

● *Below, bottom*

Winding up for the pitch in Thunder Bay.
Photographer:
Aaron Chang

● *Below, right*

On a spring day in Vancouver's east end, the men play "bocce" ball in the afternoon.
Photographer:
Jay Maisel

● *Above*

Formal wedding portrait by
Hardy Photography Studio.

● *Right*

At a wedding reception for
David Hill and the former
Peggy Aziz in Toronto, the
wedding party (and the wedding photographer) flee as the
water sprinklers suddenly
turn on.
Photographer:
Douglas Kirkland

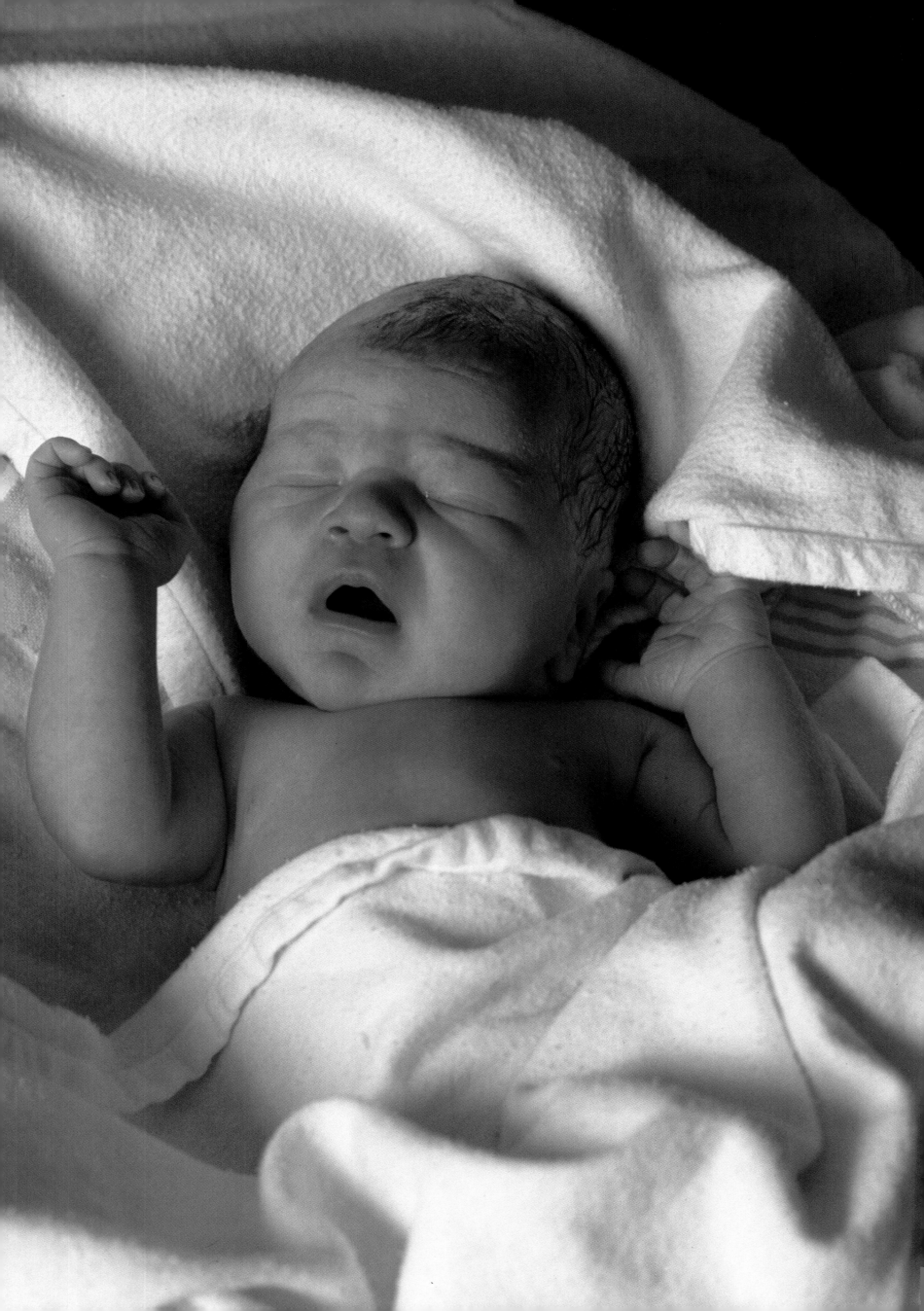

● *Left*

Ron and Carol Petrie's first child, a boy, is born at Grace Maternity Hospital in Halifax.

Photographer:
Lynn Goldsmith

● *Above*

Todd Pollack of Richard's Landing, near Sault Ste Marie, Ontario.

Photographer:
Bill DeKay

Bill Frakes

Mike Shayegani

Nicole Bengiveno

Diego Goldberg

Canadians who live in regions inhabited by polar bears both love and fear the huge animals. Here, somewhere over the Northwest Territories, photographer Sam Garcia spotted a mother with two cubs. Adult females weigh about 360 kilograms (800 pounds).

Photographer:
Sam Garcia

As twilight falls in Twillingate Harbour, these boys nimbly check the lobster pots.

Photographer:
Rudi Meisel

Drip dry in Twillingate,
Newfoundland.
Photographer:
Rudi Meisel

● *Above*

Lobster is one of the leading culinary attractions on Prince Edward Island. Tourists and locals dine side-by-side at the "New Glasgow Lobster Supper," where nearly a thousand tasty crustaceans are cracked open each night.

Photographer:
Kent Kobersteen

● *Right*

After twelve hours of ice fishing, Annie Kilruk, her husband and grandson had caught about one hundred and fifty char (a type of salmon), each weighing one to five kilograms (about two to ten pounds). Photographer Jack Corn accompanied the Kilruk family on their fishing trip.

"The sleds went slowly through the slush, throwing up huge sprays of water. Crevices in the ice were deep, and the sleds were pulled across slowly with women and children climbing off. People slipped and fell up to their waists in snow and slush, which caused great laughter."

Photographer:
Jack Corn

● *Following page*

Gill net; Prince Rupert, British Columbia. The lead line (bottom) and web (top) are lowered into the water from a fishing boat, where the net lies until it is filled with the tide's catch.

Photographer:
Al Harvey

● *Following pages 166-167*

Lobster boats moored at the wharf in Caraquet, New Brunswick.

Photographer:
Stephanie Maze

● *Following pages 168-169*

The skyline of Calgary, oil capital of Canada, rose from a fort established in 1875 by the North West Mounted Police.

Photographer:
Gary Chapman

Gary Chapman

Steve K

FOAM STATION

● *Previous page*

A worm's-eye view of Petro-Canada's SEDCO oil rig number 710.

Photographer:

Steve Krongard

● *Above*

On a Petro-Canada oil rig 200 kilometres (125 miles) off the coast of Newfoundland, a fire-fighter stands ready for action any time a helicopter lands. An average shift on the rig is three weeks of twelve-hour days. There are 105 men on this exploratory platform which has been located here for a year.

Photographer:

Steve Krongard

● *Right*

Coal miner Tom Taylor surfaces after an eight-hour shift in the Westar mine, near Fernie, British Columbia.

One of the few underground coal mines remaining in Canada, Westar plans to phase out the operation in 1987.

Mining in Canada dates back almost a millennium to the Norsemen who dug iron ore for tools from the bogs of Newfoundland. Five centuries later the French explorer Jacques Cartier mined quartz and iron pyrites thinking they were diamonds and gold.

Photographer:

Jim Wiley

Michelle Wiseman and friends watch a softball game in Uranium City, Saskatchewan. Once a flourishing mining town of 4,000 on the shores of Lake Athabasca, the town now has less than 200 inhabitants.

When uranium was found in northern Saskatchewan in the late 1940s, Eldorado Resources built a town in the wilderness to house mineworkers and their families. An entire generation was born and raised in Uranium City.

In 1982, the high grade uranium ore which was the town's lifeblood ran out. The mine was closed, and slowly, homes were abandoned and boarded up. Although there are currently no plans to search for new deposits, Uranium City's remaining inhabitants have decided to stay.

Photographer:
Chuck Fishman

● *Above, top*

Kenneth and his friends hang out on "Reggae Block" in Montreal's Jamaican neighborhood.

Photographer:

Dana Fineman

● *Above*

Over 100 years old, Fox Point Lighthouse is one of sixty-five which dot the Newfoundland coast. Wesley Pym has been the keeper for over thirty-two years. These days, both the flashing light and the foghorn are automatic. "It doesn't leave much to do but keep the station looking good," says Pym, who retires in two years.

Photographer:

Ottmar Bierwagen

● *Left*

Ottawa.

Photographer:

Gregory Heisler

● *Above, top*

Toronto.

Photographer:

Nicole Bengiveno

● *Above*

Dancing between the shadows in Toronto.

Photographer:

Nicole Bengiveno

● *Below*

9:00 PM is closing time at the Patio Bar in Wasaga Beach, Ontario.

Photographer:

Victor Fisher

● *Following page*

Prince Albert National Park, Saskatchewan.

Photographer:

Ken Gigliotti

● *Following pages 182-183*

9:00 PM on a hot, humid evening in suburban Ottawa.

Photographer:

Gregory Heisler

● *Following pages 184-185*

Port Edward, British Columbia lives on fish and timber. Here, the smokestacks of the Westar Pulp and Paper mill provide a backdrop for fishing boats in drydock.

Photographer:

Al Harvey

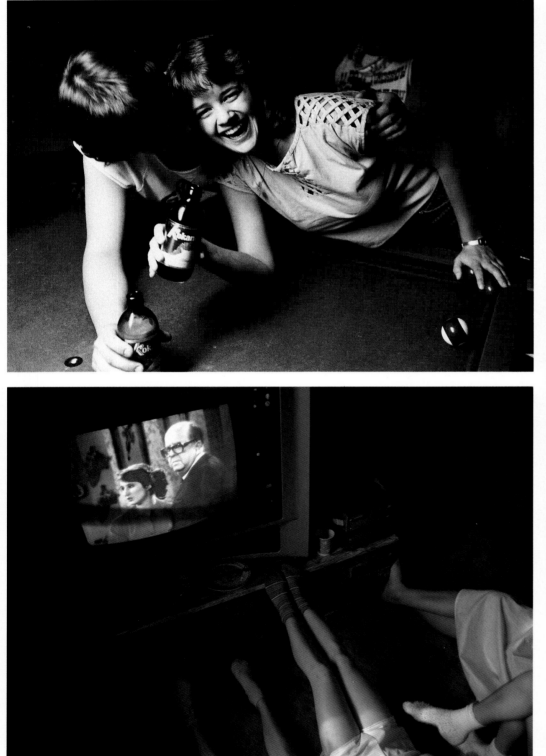

● *Above, top*

On a Friday night in Castlegar, British Columbia, a beer and someone to share it with make the perfect party.
Photographer:
Andy Levin

● *Above*

A living room in Ottawa's Rockcliffe Park.
Photographer:
Donna Ferrato

● *Right*

In the dead of a rainy night on Gottingen Street, Troy Nelson of Halifax is bound for points unknown.
Photographer:
Eli Reed

● *Left and above*

The "Frantic Follies," a showgirl revue in White-horse, Yukon, seeks to recapture the heady atmosphere of the Klondike Gold Rush days. The legendary gold rush came and went, and Whitehorse, a town of 11,000 people, now thrives on copper mining and fur trapping.

Photographer:
Tedd Church

● *Above, top*

Loading freight at Churchill
Airport, Manitoba.

Photographer:
Alex Webb

● *Above*

In St. John's, Newfoundland,
Geoff Dawe relaxes on the
stoop with his dog, Morgan.

Photographer:
Steve Krongard

● *Right*

Vancouver City Hall looks
out over the largest city in
Western Canada and the
country's chief Pacific port.
The city was named in honor
of the English explorer, Captain George Vancouver, who
travelled with Captain James
Cook and mapped most of the
British Columbia coast.

Photographer:
Jay Maisel

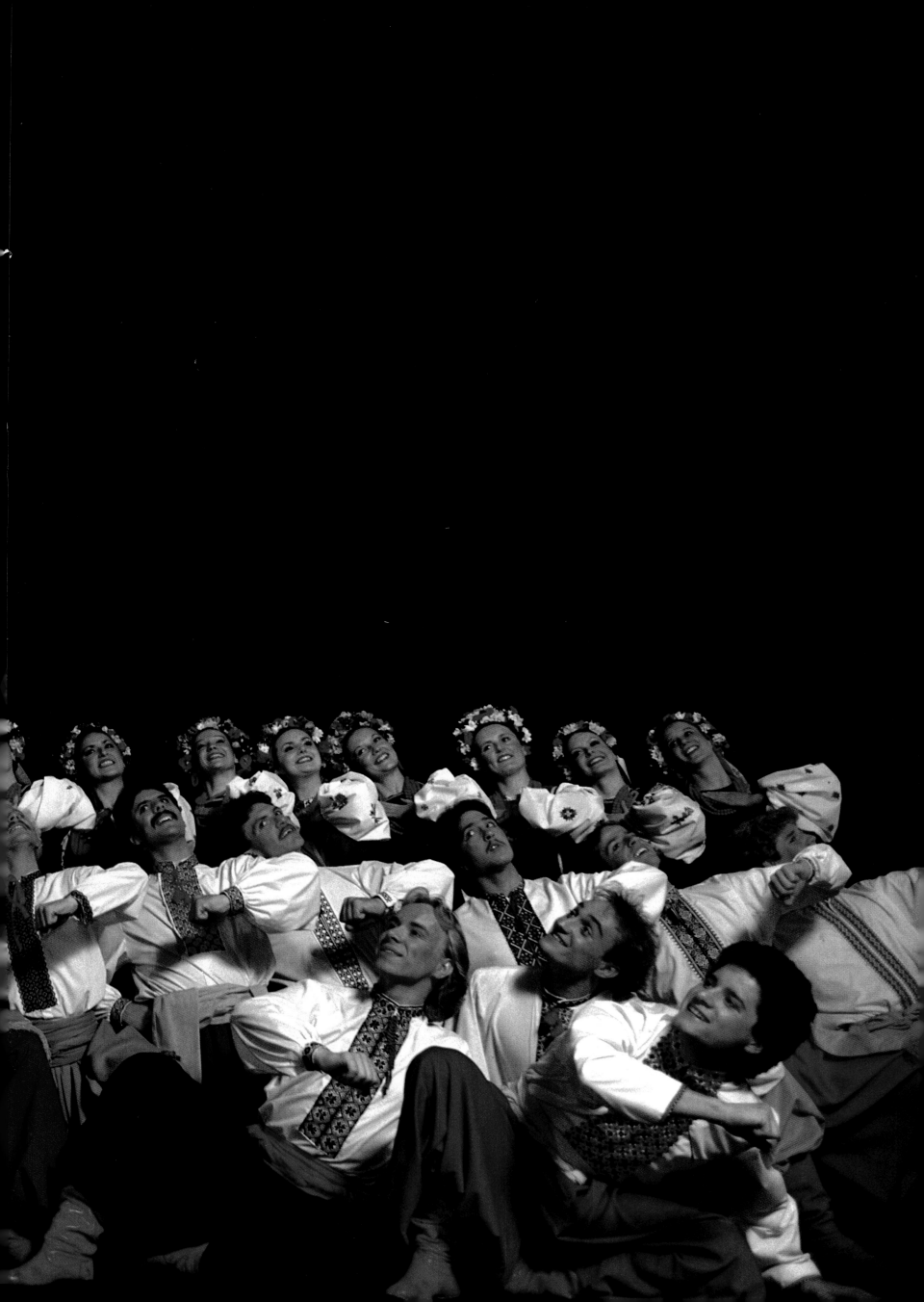

● *Previous page*

Clifton Hill, called "The Strip," is in the heart of Niagara Falls, Ontario, a bustling tourist city with a gaudy range of manmade attractions.
Photographer:
Dilip Mehta

● *Left*

Before the show at Chez Pierre in Edmonton.
Photographer:
Tom Skudra

● *Above, top and above*

In a residential neighborhood in Vancouver, the oldest profession does not work unnoticed.

The "Shame the Johns" organization, formed by West End residents who want prostitutes moved out of their neighborhood, copy customers' licence plate numbers, march in protest and otherwise disrupt business.

On June 8th, the ladies of the night staged their own counter-protest.
Photographer:
Ethan Hoffman

● *Previous page*
Officers Gerard Careen and Joe Brown patrol the docks in St. John's.

Photographer:

Frank Grant

● *Below, top*

Cam Rousselle lights up in front of the Elk River Inn, a coal miners' hangout about eight kilometres (five miles) from Fernie, British Columbia on Highway 3. Rousselle is a tireman in the maintenance shop at Line Creek Mine.

Photographer:

Jim Wiley

● *Below, bottom*

Shotaro Kajita, owner of Amandine Bakery in Calgary, presents his work.

Photographer:

Gary Chapman

● *Below*

After tipping back a few at the Cliff Hanger Bar, Don and Geoff hop the fence for a ''skinny dip'' at the Hot Springs Aqua Court in Radium Hot Springs, British Columbia.

Photographer:

Cliff Hollenbeck

● *Above*

On a night to remember, two new graduates of Calgary's Dr. Scarlett High School share a quiet moment at the senior prom.
Photographer:
Ken Heyman

● *Right*

Photographer Dilip Mehta took up position in a nearby building and used a zoom lens to capture the wonder of the ferris wheel at a Niagara Falls fairground.
Photographer:
Dilip Mehta

● *Following page*

A Day in the Life of Canada photographers pose for Steve Krongard shortly before leaving Toronto on their assignments.
Photographer:
Steve Krongard

Steve Krongard

Photographers' Assignment Locations

9:30 AM
Sydney, Nova Scotia.
Matthew Naythons

Alberta

① Banff
Audrey Topping

② Calgary
Gary Chapman
Ken Heyman
Bill Simpkins
Jim Wiley

③ Chauvin
Lynn Johnson

④ Edmonton
Bill Brooks
Tom Skudra

⑤ Fort McMurray
Alon Reininger

⑥ Jasper
Robin Moyer

⑦ Pincher Creek
P.F. Bentley

British Columbia

⑧ Harrison Hot Springs
Michael Creagon

⑨ Kelowna
Yuri Dojc

⑩ Kootenay Region
Andy Levin

⑪ Nanaimo
Arnaud de Wildenberg

⑫ Okanagan Valley
Shelly Katz

⑬ Port Edward
Al Harvey

⑭ Port Hardy
Kazuyoshi Nomachi

⑮ Radium Hot Springs
Cliff Hollenbeck

⑯ Stewart
Bill Frakes

⑰ Vancouver
Ethan Hoffman
Jay Maisel
Jim Nachtwey
Mike Shayegani

⑱ Vanderhoof
Grant Black

⑲ Victoria
Anthony Edgeworth

Manitoba

⑳ Churchill
Alex Webb

㉑ Dauphin
Hans Deryk

㉒ Flin Flon
Ken Sakamoto

㉓ Gimli
Maddy Miller

㉔ Winnipeg
Misha Erwitt
Rick Smolan

New Brunswick

㉕ Balledune
Reza

㉖ Caraquet
Stephanie Maze

㉗ Fredericton
Dick Wallace

㉘ Grand Manan Island
Gail Harvey

㉙ Moncton
Andy Clark

㉚ Saint John
Freeman Patterson

Newfoundland

㉛ Catalina
Frank Grant

㉜ Corner Brook
Vince Streano

㉝ Deer Lake
Ottmar Bierwagen

㉞ Offshore Rig
Steve Krongard

㉟ St. John's
Rudi Meisel
Boris Spremo

㊱ Stephenville
Ken Kerr

Northwest Territories

㊲ Inuvik
Dan Budnick

㊳ Magnetic pole
Sam Garcia

㊴ Pangnirtung
Jack Corn

㊵ Tuktoyaktuk
Harry Mattison

㊶ Yellowknife
Eric Hayes

Nova Scotia

㊷ Annapolis Valley
Bob Davis

㊸ Halifax
Lynn Goldsmith
Eli Reed

㊹ Pictou
Ted Grant

㊺ Sydney
Matthew Naythons

Ontario

㊻ Elmira
Andrew Stawicki

㊼ Kemptville
Roger Ressmeyer

㊽ Kenora
Colin Price

㊾ London
Peter Martin

㊿ Niagara Falls
Dilip Mehta

51 Ottawa
Gregory Heisler
John Loengard

52 Petawawa
Greg Stott

53 Peterborough
Michel Gravel

54 Polar Bear Provincial Park
Tsuneo Enari

55 Rapids, Ottawa River
Gary Hershorn

56 Rockcliffe Park
Donna Ferrato

57 Sault Ste Marie
Bill DeKay

58 Sudbury
Alan Carruthers

59 Thunder Bay
Aaron Chang

60 Tobermory
Crombie McNeill

61 Toronto
Abbas
Nicole Bengiveno
Larry Frank
Daniel Gautreau
Douglas Kirkland
Jill Krementz
Michael O'Brien

62 Wasaga Beach
Victor Fisher

Prince Edward Island

63 Charlottetown
Douglas Ball
Paul Chesley
Kent Kobersteen

Quebec

64 Anticosti Island
Pierre Gaudard

65 Gaspé
Micha Bar-Am

66 Montreal
Jennifer Erwitt
Dana Fineman
Carl Ganter
Roland Neveu

67 Quebec City
Frank Fournier

68 Schefferville
Diego Goldberg

69 St-Laurent d'Orléans
Jean-Pierre Laffont

70 St-Jean-Port-Joli
Al Normandin

71 Waterloo
Malak

Saskatchewan

72 Estevan
Gerd Ludwig

73 Prince Albert
Ken Gigliotti

74 Regina
Sherman Hines

75 Saskatoon
Debra Streuber Schulke

76 Uranium City
Chuck Fishman

Yukon Territory

77 Whitehorse
Bob Anderson
Tedd Church

Yukon
Territory

Northwest Territories

British
Columbia

Alberta

3:30 PM
Mountain wild flowers near the
Casabello Winery in Kelowna,
British Columbia.
Yuri Dojc

MIDNIGHT
By the light of the midnight sun,
Philip Kuptana prepares for an all
night muskrat hunt in the Mackenzie
River Delta.
Dan Budnick

5:00 AM
A young cormorant nests
near the Scott Paper
company in Pictou,
Nova Scotia.

4:30 PM
St. Croix Cove, Nova Scotia.

Newfoundland

Prince
Edward
Island

Saskatchewan   Manitoba

Ontario   Quebec

11:30 AM
Two friends share sun and gossip in
Toronto's Chinatown.

2:00 PM
At the Royal Canadian Mounted
Police Academy in Regina, a sergeant
major barks orders at his troops.

A Day in the Life Revisited

Chris Isfeld

It's 1974. *Life* magazine devotes a special issue to "One Day in the Life of America," and at age 24, Rick Smolan is hired at the last moment as the youngest of the 100 photographers on the project. A hundred great photographers, all recording the life of a nation on the same day. What a wonderful idea! Smolan, excited about this first major magazine assignment, can't sleep for two days. On the day itself, he is so tired that he does poorly, getting only two small pictures in the issue.

The bigger idea, though, imprinted itself on Smolan's mind. Even six years later when he was travelling the world as a freelance photographer, that first assignment continued to haunt him. He knew he could have done better and he wanted another chance. Why not a whole book about a day in the life of, say, Australia? Not only had Smolan covered Melbourne and Sydney for *Time* magazine, he had just followed a young woman and four camels 3,000 kilometres across the Gibson Desert for *National Geographic* magazine. He knew the country.

Smolan polled his photographer friends by telephone and at dinner tables around the world. They loved the idea: A band of 100 of the best—colleagues, competitors, mates—would blow in from all over the world, commune for a few days, then disperse to shoot their assignments, knowing that they were all competing for precious space in a book that would be as much about them as about Australia.

And this time, their photographs would become two-page book spreads half a metre wide, instead of postage-stamp asides to someone else's story. They

saw themselves returning from "Down Under" to Beirut, Hong Kong, Paris, the New York studios, wearing Aussie slouch hats with the side turned up like Mel Gibson in *Gallipoli.* It sounded like fun.

Publishers, however—in both Australia and the U.S.—thought Smolan was crazy. But seven years after the *Life* issue, and much to everyone's surprise, the book actually came off the presses. With the help of a young marketing whiz and former photo agency editor, David Cohen, Smolan had gone ahead and published the book on his own. "We borrowed money from everyone—families, corporations, friends—you name it," he says.

The book looked great, the photographers loved it, and it became a smash hit worldwide. In Toronto, Canada, Collins Publishers were the distributor for *A Day in the Life of Australia* but Nick Harris, the firm's president, was dreaming of other things. "I've always wanted to do a picture book about Canada," Harris says. "What I really liked about the *Australia* book was that it involved an international group of photographers as well as Australians, and achieved that rare combination of fresh eyes on the one hand and real knowledge of the country on the other. That's what gives the book such international appeal."

Harris continues, "We called in the team that did *Australia* because we wanted a book with the same appeal. Rick and David had spent years tracking down the world's best photographers. Now they had worked with them, and there was trust and confidence on both sides."

Collins made their move in November 1983. Just as Smolan and Cohen were in the thick of organizing a *Hawaii* book, Nick Harris turned up in Honolulu armed with his own enthusiasm and Collins' backing —to the tune of almost $750,000.

Those funds would cover the actual printing and promotion of a book called *A Day in the Life of Canada*. The rest of the money for the project would have to be raised by Smolan and Cohen from civic-minded Canadian companies.

There was an even bigger obstacle—time. Along with the opportunity to create what could become the most successful picture book in history came one condition: The book must be in the stores by November 1984.

In November 1983, the *Hawaii* book hadn't even been shot. To make Collins' deadline, the *Canada* book had to be at the printers by July 20, 1984. Smolan and Cohen had half a year to create two books and raise $500,000. They gulped and accepted the challenge.

By the end of March, the *Hawaii* book was finished. Smolan and Cohen dashed up to Toronto, bringing copies of the handsome *Australia* book—the only palpable proof that an idea as crazy as *A Day in the Life of Canada* could work. They waxed eloquent: "...visual time capsule...unique opportunity to define Canada through pictures...." But Corporate Canada proved to be the toughest nut the team had ever tried to crack. After six weeks of hearing that *A Day in the Life of Canada* didn't "fit in with our corporate objectives at this time," and with the project mentally written off, at the very last moment, the long jumps began to materialize.

CP Air offered free flights on its routes, bringing photographers into Canada and flying them around the country as needed. The Sheraton Centre in Toronto donated rooms and office space. Kodak provided all the film, as well as disc cameras for 100 schoolchildren to shoot their own special world on The Day. Apple Computer came up with an Apple LISA for the project staff.

Coopers & Lybrand offered their accounting skills, as they had done for *Australia* and *Hawaii*. Canon donated cash, T-shirts and, most important to the staff, a copying machine. Tilden offered discounted rental cars, Daymen Photo Marketing gave each photographer a Lowe-Pro camera bag. New York Filmworks would develop all the film. And Petro-Canada committed to crucial funding for the book.

"It's always one individual at a company who believes in the project, who works in an atmosphere where he doesn't have to worry about taking a risk," says Smolan. "That person becomes part of our team. Petro-Canada is a good example. Bill Hopper, the chairman, maintains a company where his director of corporate identity, Bill Simpkins, can champion a proposal like *A Day in the Life of Canada*."

June 8th, a Friday, was fixed for the photography. "It's the best day of the week," Smolan says. "You get people going about their normal business, then beginning to wind down for the weekend, relaxing." It was time to put the team together. Douglas Kirkland, celebrity photographer and old friend, a Canadian involved in both previous projects, agreed to act as co-director. Journalism professor and photographer Jack Corn, who looks and talks like a character from a Ma Kettle film, flew up from Tennessee to be director of photography and assignment editor. Bill Peabody on logistics, Jennifer Erwitt on materiel, Patti Richards on publicity, and Torontonians Pauline Johnson, Janet Heisey and June White completed the team. All ably assisted by six photographic arts students from Toronto's Ryerson Institute, grandly called "interns."

Project Director David Cohen slings bags filled with film, model releases, maple sugar polar bears and other essentials.

At the briefing session for photographers, Project Director Rick Smolan demonstrates a camera bag designed for the photographer who can't decide what equipment to take on assignment.

211

Gary Chapman

Logistics coordinator Bill Peabody's job is simple. He merely has to get a photographer to every place on the map where there is a dot.

Jack Corn

I couldn't speak Inuit and Mosesee didn't speak English, so we communicated with sign language. There was a light snow falling and it was very cold and windy. Mosesee carried a .22 calibre long rifle and a white screen of cloth to camouflage himself and allow him to silently creep up on a seal. He was the most naturally patient man I've ever met. Three times during the course of the night, he approached a seal. The first time, the seal heard us and slid through a hole in the ice. The second time, he wounded the seal, but it got away. Several hours went by and we were about to give up, when Mosesee spotted a third seal very close to us. He only had time to fire one shot and it hit the seal in the head. It headed for a hole in the ice but died before it got there. The seal weighed about 85 pounds, and I had my first taste of raw seal meat that night.

In offices set up at the Sheraton Centre, opposite Toronto's City Hall, the game was on. The first task: To induce 100 leading photojournalists to drop whatever they were doing and come to Canada on incredibly short notice for one day of concentrated shooting. *A Day in the Life of Canada*—soon known as *DITLOCA*—wanted at least forty to be Canadians. As word spread, the names came flooding in. And what about the others—the French, British, Americans, Japanese, Germans? Many had worked on the *Australia* book, many on *Hawaii*, a few on both. And there is always new talent. The list grew.

Next, how to find the devils! Shooters are nomads, jetting from country to country to shoot battles and elections, fashion and film stars. "This is nothing like doing a conventional book," Smolan says. "It's more like making a movie. You're finding locations, getting the cast together, soothing the stars. And on The Day, it's like directing one big crowd scene. By now, David and I think we know how George Lucas and Steven Spielberg feel!"

But the photographers were found, by telephone, by telegram, by bullying their employers or their families. They would be getting a small honorarium

for their day's work and nothing for the time they'd spend travelling. They'd have to pay for their own cabs and coffees and doughnuts. But most answered: "Are you kidding? Of course I'll be there!"

The palatial lobby of the Sheraton Centre had rarely seen the likes of these travellers. They came in various combinations of war zone chic—flak jackets, bush jackets, denim jackets and fatigues. They wore running shoes, hiking boots, combat boots, even French gardening boots. Eli Reed arrived from El Salvador, Abbas from Beirut, Robin Moyer from Afghanistan. They all walked with that strange, lopsided gait that comes from moving about the world with a camera bag slung from one shoulder.

They embraced each other like refugees suddenly lifted from a battlefield. And so they were—refugees from pressure-packed assignments and frantic deadlines. Rather than cover the world's news that day, they were together to explore a nation's soul, wherever they found it.

Smolan and Cohen were ecstatic. The whole project, on the brink of disaster after harrowing weeks of too little funding, too many photographers, too big a

Gary Chapman

The staff: (Seated, left to right) David Cohen, Susan Kivi, June White, Bill DeKay, Pat Tagiolini, Rick Smolan, and Vivian Chapman. (Standing, left to right) Jack Corn, Mandy Heisey, Victor Fisher, Bill Peabody, Patti Richards, Rick Upton, Jennifer Erwitt, Rosalie Favell, and Pauline Johnson.

At dawn, Director of
Photography Jack Corn jogs
around Toronto's City Hall.

Great Canadians: Boris
Spremo of *The Toronto Star*,
Michel Gravel of *La Presse*,
and Frank Grant of G/W
Photography Ltd.

Iranian photographer Reza
poses with the one that didn't
get away.

country, and too little time, had shifted into automatic. "It's going to be our best book yet," Cohen said. "Up to now everything has been on our shoulders. Now everything depends on the photographers. It's up to them now."

Cohen had some thoughts on the group of men and women invited to work on the project. "Photojournalism has to be the greatest form of delayed adolesence ever invented. These are people who never settle down and often never grow up, which is sometimes a problem if you are the one who has to handle their problems. But they also retain the good things about being young. They look at the world in a unique way, with an almost childlike curiosity. They don't seem to age the same way as other people. I guess I consider myself an honorary photojournalist. I've never been a working photographer but I identify very strongly with the group. I love working with photographers. I can't think of another group of people who are more interesting, exciting or kind."

DITLOCA's Patti Richards reported that newspapers, TV and radio across the country would carry stories about The Day, the CBC alone sending out eight camera crews with the photographers. Communities would greet the shooters like long lost children.

On the walls of the hotel's Essex Ballroom were proofs of pages from the yet-to-be-published *Hawaii* book. The photographers stared at them hungrily, squinting at the picture credits, keeping score. And of course, they all wanted to know about their Canada assignments. "Do I have to go back to Montreal?" asked Michel Gravel of that city's *La Presse*. "That's what my ticket says. I thought I was spending the day in a prison."

"Forget the ticket—go to the jail," said Jack Corn.

"Do not pass Go. Do not collect $200," a wag intoned.

"Of course, they all wanted to photograph Eskimos. I mean Inuit," Jack Corn said, his Tennessee accent

smooth as bourbon. "Canada is something of a blurry country to foreigners. A lot of people still think of it in terms of Sergeant Preston of the Yukon." Corn kept one of the prized "Far North" assignments for himself. Another went to Pulitzer Prize winner Jay Dickman, who had just flown in from Rome.

Corn explained the subtle artistry of assigning: "At first we tried to match photographers with assignments, but it was working out all wrong, and we didn't have time to mess with it. So we took a map and, starting in Newfoundland, assigned the locations Canadian-foreign-Canadian-foreign, until we got to the west coast."

That Monday night, June 4th, the Metro Chairman and the Mayor of Toronto hosted an outdoor party by the waterfall in the middle of the Sheraton Centre. It was windy but the sky was clear, the canapés tasty and spirits high.

Next morning came the briefing—part of the two-day process of transforming 100 individual photojournalists into a team. Rick Smolan first reminded them

Ken Heyman

I stopped for lunch around 1:30, and noticed this handsome young kid in an army camouflage jacket. He was sitting with a young girl and feeding a 6-week-old baby. There was something tender about the scene. It turned out he was in high school and lived with his parents. The girl and the baby lived with her parents. I had the feeling they were meeting surreptitiously in this Wendy's Hamburger place. He was feeding the baby with a little bottle, and he told me his only source of income was from the weekend army reserve unit he belonged to. He was so shy that he couldn't say yes or no when I asked him if he minded my taking pictures of him and the baby. He just shrugged and seemed sort of overwhelmed by my question and by life in general. When I asked him to write his address so I could send him some pictures, his writing was tiny, minuscule.

It all started four years ago
when photographer Gregory
Heisler married Prudence
Taubert during the *Day in the
Life of Australia* project. Here,
photographer Shelly Katz of
Dallas surprises Kathy Whalen
by proposing on their first night
in Toronto.

Gary Chapman

Gary Chapman

Alon Reininger

Israeli photographer Alon Reininger in the mirror of a 500 tonne digging machine at the Syncrude surface mine in Alberta.

Time magazine photographer P.F. Bentley with the latest style in camera bags.

Steve Krongard coaxes a smile out of 99 fellow photographers while taking the *DITLOCA* group portrait.

Gail Harvey

Grand Manan is an unspoiled fishing island cut off from the rest of the world. The only way to get to the island is on a ferry which runs only three times a week. There are 2,500 people on Grand Manan, and they all seem to be related. I think there are only six last names on the entire island. The place was like a spider web, and after spending a little time there, you start to see that the whole community is interconnected. If you speak to one person, you touch one end of the spider web and on the other side of the island someone else jumps.

I met an old man on Grand Manan named Leland Wilcox who writes hymns and poems that God sends him. Apparently, four years ago, he woke up his wife in the middle of the night and said, "God has sent me a song. Quick, get a paper and pencil." She rolled over and looked at him and said, "If God is sending you songs, then he can send you a damn pencil, too."

that they must get the people they photographed to sign model releases. "Do you want us to take pictures or negotiate contracts?" came a voice from the back. Smolan went on: "You're not here to photograph the rich, famous and powerful. Or to make picture postcards. Your job is to create a visual time capsule, a book which people can look at forty years from now and say, 'This is what it was like to live in Canada in 1984.' Our goal is to make extraordinary pictures of ordinary events."

Smolan shared a few other thoughts with the group. "We are here for two reasons; to have fun and to be creative at the same time. Sometimes we get so caught up in our day-to-day assignments that we never really have a chance to reflect on what we are doing with our lives, with our photographs. One of my goals with the *Day in the Life* projects is to give each of you a chance to catch your breath, to spend time with other photographers whom you admire and respect, to exchange ideas and information, and to apply your creativity to a unique place in a collaborative way."

John Durniak, former picture editor of *The New York Times* and *Time* magazine, reminded the photographers that Canada wasn't all pine trees and polar bears. "This is a country of philosophers, writers and musicians," he said, reading off a long list of Canadian accomplishments.

Durniak had also drawn the unenviable task of bullying one hundred very independent souls into writing decent captions, taking the time to get down on paper the names, numbers and facts without missing the decisive moment with their cameras. "If you can't get good captions and good stories, you're not a good journalist and if you don't come back with interesting pictures in a country with so much variety you're just not an interesting person," said the bearded 220-pound bear of a picture editor. The crowd grew restless, but no one would challenge the man who gave half of the photographers in the room their first real assignments. "Risk your professional reputations," he told them. "You have the opportunity to become part of the cultural history of Canada."

Back in the *DITLOCA* offices, co-ordinator Bill Peabody crouched before his Apple LISA computer and his Wang word processor, working on last-minute logistics. How to get Sam Garcia to the north magnetic pole and Chuck Fishman to Uranium City, a new ghost town in northern Saskatchewan. And how to get Jack Corn to Pangnirtung on Baffin Island. More important—how to get him to *pronounce* Pangnirtung.

Corn got there by flying to Montreal, then to Frobisher Bay, about 350 kilometres southwest of Pang, as the locals call it (much to Corn's relief). From Frobisher Bay, he flew some 800 kilometres north of Pang to Pond Inlet. Then back south to his destination.

As for Sam Garcia, his problem was both getting to the magnetic pole *and* finding it. It moves around constantly. The *DITLOCA* staff presented him with a handful of paperclips so he could do some Mr. Wizard experiments when—or if—he did get there.

Bill DeKay

At the Kodak Children's Workshop, famous photographers teach Toronto school children how to use disc cameras.

214

Matthew Naythons takes a self-portrait in the washroom of a coal mine in Sydney, Nova Scotia.

Canadian Photographer of the Year Dilip Mehta finds a unique vantage point for his picture story on world famous Niagara Falls.

A young student from King Edward public school practises using his disc camera at the Kodak Children's Workshop in Toronto.

On Wednesday, June 6th, the shooters left for their assignments. Boris Spremo headed for St. John's, Newfoundland, hoping to get the book's first sunrise. Malak headed for an artists' colony near Montreal. Douglas Kirkland went to stay with his parents in Fort Erie, Ontario.

Most of the photographers were billeted with obliging families. "We couldn't afford hotels," Cohen says. "But it also gave the photographers a more intimate view of the country. In Hawaii, they stayed in hotels, and we missed a lot of good pictures: Families waking up, having breakfast, watching TV at night, the small moments, unnoticed in context, which can be discovered through photography."

In Toronto, Thursday was sunny and warm. But on the road, the photographers were having problems and would complain about rain and fog and haze when they got back. "There are no mountains in Banff," said Robin Moyer, assigned to the Rockies. "But they do have fog, and rain. I couldn't see a damn thing."

Boris Spremo spent the night in a lighthouse at Cape Spear, Canada's easternmost point, and did a 4 AM wake-up in hopes of getting his sunrise. As he and the lighthouse keeper waited, three shadowy figures appeared, climbing the rocks toward them. In his thirty-odd years on the job, the keeper had never seen anything like it. Spremo thought he was about to get a unique picture. But the three climbers turned out to be a CBC camera crew coming to film Spremo's shoot.

In Warkworth prison, Michel Gravel found that he had to spend more time on official paperwork than on taking pictures. Rick Smolan was flying over Winnipeg with the Snowbirds, the Canadian Forces aerobatic team. "We did so many rolls and turns keeping up with the rest of the jets, we hit 4Gs (four times gravity)," he said. "The pilots love to do numbers on journalists. Mine said that the writers throw up, but photographers usually don't."

At an Ontario steel mill, young intern Bill DeKay was producing a top-notch photo essay that would rival the work of some of the "real photographers." Part of the *Day in the Life* tradition has been to pass the torch on to the next generation of talented photographers. DeKay's work exemplifies this.

Douglas Kirkland stood alongside the official photographer at a society wedding on a vast Toronto lawn. When the sprinkler system suddenly came on, the wedding party and the official photographer fled. Bridesmaids in formal dresses tumbled laughing on the ground. The bride trailed a sodden train through the grass. Kirkland squeezed off three fast frames and got the picture.

In Ottawa, Donna Ferrato, working without prior clearances, was turned away at one ambassador's residence after another, until she finally got into the Saudi chancery. "It was beautiful," she says. "Like a museum." But Ferrato's best pictures were early morning and evening shots of the family with whom she stayed. Classic *Day in the Life* pictures.

Jay Maisel captures a flight of fancy in Vancouver's Stanley Park.

While on assignment in a Toronto mannequin factory, photographer Michael O'Brien of *Life* magazine (right) poses with a new friend (left).

French photographer Arnaud de Wildenberg strikes a pose for American photographer Gregory Heisler.

These twenty-two eyes edited 110,000 pictures in three days. (Front row, left to right) Jack Corn, Maddy Miller, Elisabeth Biondi, Melissa Duffner, Woody Camp, (Back row, left to right) Ethan Hoffman, Brigitte Barkley, Christiane Breustedt, Leslie Smolan, and Kent Kobersteen. Captain Action on the far right is Steve Pigeon of Masterfile.

Sam Garcia

I thought I was going to a place called the North Magnetic Pole, but I found out that it's not a specific spot, it actually moves around.

When we got off the plane, I started to walk away, but the pilot said, "I really don't think you should go anywhere until I load my gun." I could see thirty miles in every direction. The view was amazing, a vast empty whiteness to the horizon, absolutely clear and flat. I said, "Come on, you can see for miles." He said, "I'm not kidding," and stayed by my side the whole time. He didn't take his eyes off the horizon for a second. That day I saw five polar bears. Now, if you have trouble seeing one on a bright sunny day, can you imagine working on a rig when it's minus forty degrees in a blizzard and wondering the whole time if there's a 1,000-pound bear sneaking up on you?

At the base camp there's a sign on the door: "Warning. Do NOT assume there is NOT a polar bear outside this door." They mean it very seriously. A couple of days before, some guy was attacked and his arm almost torn off. He had gone out that same door, and met a polar bear.

In Hull, Quebec, Roger Ressmeyer from San Francisco found himself on his last shoot of the day, at the Miss Nude Ottawa-Hull contest. "I've never shot nudes before," he said. "Actually, my father's a minister. Both my grandfathers were ministers. I don't know what they'll say." To let him know when he had to stop shooting, when the 24 hours were over, Ressmeyer had set his digital wristwatch alarm for midnight. It went off in the middle of the Miss Nude show, playing "Jesu, Joy of Man's Desiring."

On Saturday, the photographers started to return. They handed in their film, captions and model releases. Douglas Kirkland, Pauline Johnson and Amy Schiffman (*American Photographer* magazine) debriefed them. They described their Day, trying to recall their best shots. They liked their families and found that they were known and welcomed, even in the small towns, because of the project's tremendous publicity. Most claimed to have brought back "interesting images." Some were interviewed on videotape for the documentary film about *DITLOCA*. Exhaustion blended with exhilaration.

That night the Sheraton Centre put on a barbecue by the waterfall to say farewell to the photographers. Everybody applauded the hotel's David Hamilton and

Hans Gerhardt and at 7:20, a light plane flew over trailing a banner that read: Sheraton Salutes *A Day in the Life of Canada!!*

A strange mood descended over the crowd. The laughter died down and voices were lowered. The photographers took some pictures of each other. The project was ending and the group was about to go its separate ways. For a few days on the *DITLOCA* project they'd been able to lay aside professional competitiveness, share secrets of the trade, and be together as a "family." Now the family was breaking up. They had all shared the incredible experience of turning an ordinary day into something extraordinary by preserving it forever on film.

At the height of confusion on The Day, Smolan surveyed the scene and said, "Imagine that the cameras don't jam, imagine that 100 photographers actually manage to piece together what happened in Canada today. OK, now imagine a few generations down the road, when things have changed. Imagine what this book might say and the forgotten memories that these pictures will recall. Just imagine that."

Michael Hanlon
The Toronto Star

Marijke Leupen, picture editor of *Maclean's*, and Bob Carroll, picture editor of United Press Canada, at the farewell party at the Sheraton Centre.

DITLOCA production assistant Kai Sanburn and Eli Reed of the Magnum photo agency edit pictures shot on The Day.

Photographers' Biographies

Abbas

A Day in the Life of Hawaii   1983

Abbas
Iranian/Paris, France
A member of the prestigious Magnum agency, Abbas has covered Africa, the Middle East and Asia for the past ten years. He completed a one year study of Mexico in 1984.

Bob Anderson
Canadian/Ottawa, Ontario
Anderson was born in Glasgow, Scotland and moved to Canada in 1974. A specialist in corporate and industrial photography, his work is included in the collection of the National Film Board and in the National Photography Collection in the Public Archives of Canada.

Douglas Ball
Canadian/Montreal, Quebec
Once a semi-professional hockey player, Ball is now a leading news photographer working for Canadian Press in Montreal. He has won twelve Canadian Press Picture of the Month Awards, two Picture of the Year Awards and, in 1974 and 1977, National Newspaper Awards.

Micha Bar-am
Israeli/Jerusalem, Israel
Bar-am's career has spanned the many wars and dramatic events in the Middle East which he has covered for *The New York Times, The Washington Post, Time, Newsweek, Stern, The Times* (London) and *American Photographer*. He has also published books and exhibited widely in Israel and the United States.

Nicole Bengiveno
American/San Francisco, California
A staff photographer for the San Francisco *Examiner* since 1977, Bengiveno was named 1979 News Photographer of the Year by the San Francisco Press Photographers Association.

P. F. Bentley
American/New York, New York
Since 1976, Bentley has been a contributor to *Newsweek, The New York Times, USA Today* and *Time*. He covered the 1984 U.S. presidential campaign for *Time*.

Ottmar Bierwagen

Ontario   1980

Ottmar Bierwagen
Canadian/Calgary, Alberta
Winner of the Ontario News Photographer of the Year Award in 1978 and 1979, Bierwagen was photography director for the *Winnipeg Free Press* and staff photographer for *The Toronto Sun*. His work can also be seen regularly in *National Geographic*.

Grant Black
Canadian/Windsor, Ontario
Black is a native of Deloraine, Manitoba, with a degree in print journalism from Loyalist College. Among other awards, he has won the 1978 Canadian Weekly Newspaper Association Best Feature Picture and a Canadian Press Picture of the Month Award. His work has appeared in *The Windsor Star, Chatelaine* and *Maclean's*.

Bill Brooks
Canadian/Scarborough, Ontario
Before becoming a freelance photographer in 1972, Brooks was photo editor at the McClelland and Stewart Ltd. publishing company and studio manager at Ashley and Crippen, Toronto. He has published ten picture books on Canadian subjects.

Dan Budnick
American/New Mexico
Budnick has worked for many of the world's leading publications including *National Geographic, Life, Newsweek, Time, Fortune, GEO, L'Express, Paris-Match* and *Stern*. He has also photographed annual reports for many leading international corporations.

Alan Carruthers

Equinox magazine   1984

Alan Carruthers
Canadian/Sudbury, Ontario
Born in England, Carruthers began his career in photography in 1973, two years after his arrival in Canada. He has freelanced for most major Canadian magazines and several commercial clients including Air Canada, Canada Steamship Lines, Nabisco and the Royal Canadian Mint.

Aaron Chang

Hawaii   1983

Aaron Chang
American/Honolulu, Hawaii
Since 1979, Chang has been senior staff photographer for *Surfing* magazine. In 1982, he received the American Society of Magazine Photographers Award of Excellence. He was named one of the five best sports photographers in the U.S. by *American Photographer* magazine. His work has also appeared in *Stern*, French *Vogue* and *GQ*.

Gary Chapman

Florida   1978

Gary Chapman
American/Louisville, Kentucky
Chapman is currently a staff photographer for *The Courier Journal* and the *Times* in Louisville, Kentucky. His work has appeared in *Time, Forbes* and *Sports Illustrated*. He was one of the 100 *Day in the Life of Australia* photographers.

Paul Chesley
American/Aspen, Colorado
A freelance photographer based in Aspen, Chesley is a regular contributor to *National Geographic, GEO, Time* and other publications. Solo exhibitions of his work have been held in the U.S. and Japan, including a 1984 show at the Academy of Arts in Honolulu.

Tedd Church
Canadian/Montreal, Quebec
Church has won two National Newspaper Awards and six Canadian Press awards.

Andy Clark
Canadian/Ottawa, Ontario
Clark started in the news photography business in 1970 as a copyboy in the picture department of Canadian Press in Toronto. He has worked for the Hamilton *Spectator* and, since 1979, for United Press Canada for whom he has travelled the world covering news events.

Jack Corn

Tennessee   1963

Jack Corn
American/Nashville, Tennessee
One of the senior figures in American news photography, Corn's work has appeared in *Time, The New York Times, Life, The Philadelphia Inquirer*, Associated Press and United Press International. The recipient of many awards for photojournalism, Corn was Director of Photography for *Day in the Life of Canada*.

Michael Creagon
Canadian/Halifax, Nova Scotia
Born in Japan, Creagon has worked as a mining-camp-cook, scrapyard laborer, film-maker and in a factory. Since 1980, he has earned his living as a freelance photographer. He joined United Press Canada in September 1982 as the Halifax bureau picture stringer.

Bob Davis
Australian/Hong Kong
Davis travels extensively for editorial, advertising and corporate photo assignments. He has won several CLIO awards for his corporate photography. A collection of his black and white photographs was published in the book *Faces of Japan*.

Bill DeKay
Canadian/Toronto, Ontario
A recent graduate of Ryerson Polytechnical Institute, DeKay works as a cub photographer for *The London* (Ontario) *Free Press*. He was an intern on the *Day in the Life of Canada* project.

Hans Deryk
Canadian/Montreal, Quebec
Born in Holland, Deryk emigrated to Canada in 1962. He worked for four major Canadian daily newspapers before joining United Press Canada in 1982. His work includes sports, news and feature photography.

Arnaud de Wildenberg

A Day in the Life of Australia   1981

Arnaud de Wildenberg
French/Paris, France
De Wildenberg is best known for his coverage of the Afghanistan crisis and Iranian and Cambodian refugees. He won the *Paris-Match* contest for the best news report in 1980 for his work in Uganda and an award from the World Press Photo Foundation for his coverage of Lech Walesa of Poland. De Wildenberg speaks English with the funniest French accent since Frank Fournier.

Jay Dickman
American/Dallas, Texas
A photographer with *The Dallas Times-Herald*, Dickman won the Pulitzer Prize for feature photography for work done in El Salvador in 1983 and in the same year won the World Press Photo News Feature Series Gold Medal. His work has appeared in *National Geographic, Time, Life, Stern* and most other major magazines.

British Columbia   1984

Yuri Dojc
Canadian/Toronto, Ontario
Originally from Czechoslovakia, Dojc is based in Toronto where he has produced award winning annual reports and innovative fashion and product photographs. He has received prizes and awards from the Nikon and Hasselblad corporations and has appeared in *Photographis* and *Graphis Poster, The Art Annual* and *Creativity*.

Anthony Edgeworth
American/New York, New York
Edgeworth was named Color Photographer of the Year by the American Society of Magazine Photographers in 1982. He is currently a freelance photojournalist whose work has appeared in *Fortune, Life, Look,* and French *Vogue* and a commercial photographer for Chrysler, DeBeers, Ralph Lauren, Nikon and Polaroid.

Japan   1983

Tsuneo Enari
Japanese/Tokyo, Japan
Enari worked as a photojournalist for the *Mainichi* newspaper in Tokyo from 1962 to 1974.

He has won prizes from the Photographic Society of Japan and from the Kimura Ihei. He is a graduate of the Tokyo College of Economics.

Jennifer Erwitt
American/San Francisco, California
Erwitt served as production manager for the *Day in the Life of Canada* project. Her photographs have appeared in the *New York Daily News, Frets Magazine* and *Day in the Life of Hawaii*.

New York   1978

Misha Erwitt
American/New York, New York
A native New Yorker, Erwitt has been taking pictures since he was eleven. After a long stint in the film business, Erwitt took up editorial photography. He has been published in *American Photographer, Esquire* and *USA Today*.

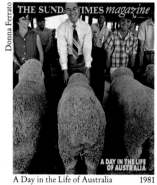
A Day in the Life of Australia   1981

Donna Ferrato
Venusian/New York, New York
A visitor from outer space, Ferrato is associated with Visions Photo Group. Her work has appeared in *Life, Newsweek* and *Bunte*, among others. She is Fanny Ferrato's mother.

Dana Fineman
American/Los Angeles, California
Fineman, twenty-three, studied photography at the Art Center College of Design in Pasadena and worked for several years as an assistant to well-known celebrity photographer Douglas Kirkland. Fineman's work appears frequently in *People, American Health* and *American Photographer*. Based in Los Angeles, Fineman is associated with the Sygma Photo Agency.

Chuck Fishman
American/New York, New York
Fishman has produced cover stories for *Life, Time, Fortune,* the *Economist* and the *Sunday Times* (London). His work has been exhibited in major galleries in the U.S. and Europe. In 1983 and 1984 he won World Press Photo Awards. He has worked on book projects in Papua, New Guinea and in Singapore.

Frank Fournier
French/New York, New York
Fournier's work has appeared in a broad array of magazines and journals, including *Paris-Match, Forbes, Le Figaro, Time* and *The New York Times Magazine*. He has extensively covered the Pope's travels in Europe and Central America, the dancer Mikhail Baryshnikov and the conflict in Lebanon. He is a member of Contact Press Images.

Cuba   1983

Bill Frakes
American/Miami, Florida
A *Miami Herald* staff member since 1979, Frakes has won numerous awards including the 1983 Overseas Press Club's Citation for Excellence and the World Press Photo Gold Medal. In 1982 he was named the U.S. Newspaper Photographer of the Year, won the Heywood Broun Award and a Robert F. Kennedy Journalism Award.

Larry Frank
Canadian/Toronto, Ontario
Originally a film-maker/photographer in New York where he worked with *Esquire* and Lippincott Publishing, Frank currently runs the Nikon School of Photography in Canada. He also teaches portraiture at Sheridan College in Oakville, Ontario.

J. Carl Ganter
American/Traverse City, Michigan
The youngest member of the DITLOCA team, Ganter is a junior at Northwestern University. An enterprising young man, Ganter managed to get U.S. Secret Service press credentials before he was fifteen. His work has appeared in *The Detroit News* and the Dutch magazine, *Der Tijd*. He is an associate member of Contact Press Images.

Sam Garcia
American/New York, New York
Garcia, formerly an Atlanta-based freelance photographer, is Special Projects Manager for Nikon working out of New York. For Nikon, he has covered space launches, the Kentucky Derby, the Indianapolis 500, and the Summer Olympic Games in Los Angeles.

Pierre Gaudard
Canadian/Montreal, Quebec
Born in France, Gaudard has lived in Canada since 1952 where he has been an award winning freelance photographer. He has received the Gold Medal from the National Film Board for photographic excellence and has exhibited his work widely in Canada and in Europe.

Manitoba   1984

Ken Gigliotti
Canadian/Winnipeg, Manitoba
Gigliotti has worked as a news photographer for the Thunder Bay *Chronicle Journal* and *Times-News* and for the *Winnipeg Free Press*. In 1981 he was named Photographer of the Year by the

Ontario News Photographers' Association. Currently, he is working on a book about the Manitoba Interlake area.

West Germany   1979

Diego Goldberg
Argentine/New York, New York
After starting photojournalism in Latin America as a correspondent for Camera Press, Goldberg moved to the Paris office in 1977, and then to New York in 1980. Now with Sygma Photo Agency, his work has been featured in major magazines throughout the world. In 1984 he won a World Photo Competition prize.

Lynn Goldsmith
American/New York, New York
Goldsmith's work has appeared in most of the world's major publications. Primarily known for her album covers and rock and roll work, she has worked for Carly Simon, Michael Jackson, Bruce Springsteen and Mick Jagger among others. Multi-talented, she is also a recording and video artist under the name Will Powers.

India   1982

Frank Grant
Canadian/Toronto, Ontario
A former staff photographer for *The Toronto Star*, Grant was named Canadian Professional Photographer of the Year in 1972. He has won over forty awards and currently specializes in annual reports and location photography with a strong editorial viewpoint.

Ted Grant
Canadian/Victoria, B.C.
Personal photographer to many political figures including former Prime Minister Joe Clark, Grant has shot sports and commercial subjects as well as politicians. His work has appeared in Canada's major magazines and newspapers and in several books about Canada. His many awards include both the Gold and Silver medals for photographic excellence from the National Film Board.

Michel Gravel
Canadian/Montreal, Quebec
Since 1954, Gravel has been on the staffs of the Montreal *Herald, Le Devoir,* the *Gazette* and *La Presse.* He has covered both local and international events and has been named Canadian Photographer of the Year.

Al Harvey
Canadian/Toronto, Ontario
A photographer whose work has been featured in several award winning audio-visual presentations, Harvey's pictures have appeared in *Maclean's, Canadian Living* and *Reader's Digest* among other magazines.

Toronto 1984

Gail Harvey
Canadian/Toronto, Ontario
Harvey has been a professional photographer for ten years. She freelances for major magazines and her work has appeared in *Maclean's, Time, Newsweek* and *People.* She has also been Director of Photography for the Toronto Film Festival.

England 1969

Eric Hayes
Canadian/Jordan Falls, Nova Scotia
A native of British Columbia, Hayes now lives in a passive solar home in Nova Scotia. During his twenty-one years as a photographer, his work has appeared in *Rolling Stone, Maclean's, The Toronto Star,* and *Harper's Bazaar,* among others. He was the winner of the 1983 National Magazine Award for Photojournalism.

A Day in the Life of Australia 1981

Gregory Heisler
American/New York, New York
Heisler was the toilet captain at Timber Elementary School in Evanston, Illinois before becoming photography editor of the Evanston High School *Key.* Since then, magazines such as *Life, GEO, Fortune, Connoisseur* and *Time* have published his photographs. Heisler produced the last two performance books of the American Ballet Theatre and hopes to do more fashion photography in the near future.

Gary Hershorn
Canadian/Toronto, Ontario
Hershorn, twenty-six, learned to use a camera while working on his school newspaper and his first published picture clinched his career choice. Since 1979 he has worked for United Press Canada covering many major national events.

Ken Heyman
American/New York, New York
For twenty-three years Heyman was Margaret Mead's photographer. He has won the World Understanding Award from Nikon and the University of Missouri and has exhibited his work on four continents. Of his fourteen published books, the most recent is *The World's Family.*

Sherman Hines
Canadian/Toronto, Ontario
One of 40 members of Camera Craftsmen, Hines lives in both Halifax and Toronto. His many awards include being the second Canadian to receive a fellowship in the American Society of Photographers. A leading exponent of environmental photography, he has published numerous books on the Canadian provinces.

Life magazine 1980

Ethan Hoffman
American/New York, New York
Hoffman won the 1980 World Understanding Award for his photo essay on Washington State Prison. His work has appeared in *Life, GEO, The New York Times, Stern, Paris-Match* and the *Daily Telegraph* (London). His new book on Japan will be out in 1985.

Cliff Hollenbeck
American/Seattle, Washington
Hollenbeck specializes in travel and advertising photography and was named Travel Photographer of the Year in 1983. His work has been published by *National Geographic, Travel & Leisure, Sunset* and other major magazines.

Lynn Johnson
American/Pittsburgh, Pennsylvania
As a contract photographer for Black Star since 1982, Johnson has been shooting for *Life, Newsweek, Forbes* and *Fortune.* Earlier, she spent seven years as a staff photographer for *The Pittsburgh Press* during which time she won seven Golden Quill Awards.

Shelly Katz
American/Dallas, Texas
A *Time* contract photographer, Katz has lived in Dallas since 1965. Born in New York City, he sold his first picture to the *New York Daily News* at age eleven. Since then, his assignments have ranged from the space program to presidential campaigns to Brooke Shields. His hobby, breaking horses, made him a natural choice for an assignment on a ranch in Canada.

Ken Kerr
Canadian/Toronto, Ontario
Kerr worked at several Toronto area weeklies for six years before joining the staff at *The Toronto Sun,* where he's been for two and a half years. Kerr was named the 1983 Ontario News Photographers' Association Photographer of the Year.

Los Angeles 1962

Douglas Kirkland
Canadian/Los Angeles, California
Kirkland is one of the world's best known glamor and personality photographers. Twenty-three years in the business include camera work with Marilyn Monroe, Judy Garland, Barbra Streisand and Christie Brinkley. Based in Los Angeles, he is one of the founding members of Contact Press Images and Co-Director of the *Day in the Life of Canada* project.

Kent Kobersteen
American/Washington, D.C.
Before joining *National Geographic* as illustrations editor in 1983, Kobersteen was staff photographer at the *Minneapolis Tribune,* a job which took him to over twenty countries primarily in Africa, the Middle East and Asia. He has won several awards from the Overseas Press Club of America as well as the 1982 World Hunger Media Award for Photography.

Jill Krementz
American/New York, New York
Highly acclaimed for her portraits of literary figures, Krementz is also a documentary photographer and author. Her work appears regularly in *The New York Times, Life, People, Newsweek* and *New York Magazine.* She has published several books of photography and her photographs are in the permanent collection of the Museum of Modern Art.

Steve Krongard
American/New York, New York
Krongard works primarily in color. His photographs were included in *Glimpses of America,* the first American color photography shown in the People's Republic of China. His advertising clients include American Airlines, British Airways, Kodak and Polaroid. His work has also appeared in *GEO* and *Fortune.*

Jean-Pierre Laffont
French/New York, New York
Laffont attended the prestigious School of Graphic Arts in Vevey, Switzerland prior to serving in the French Army in Algeria in the early 1960s. He has served as the New York correspondent for Reporters Associates and the Gamma Photo Agency. Since 1973, he has been a partner of the Sygma Photo Agency based in New York. His work appears regularly in the world's leading news magazines.

Andy Levin
American/New York, New York
Levin is a talented color technician who is well known for his photographs of New York. He is published regularly in *New York Magazine* and in *Signature,* for whom he has travelled the world. He is associated with the Black Star photo agency.

219

Life magazine   1984

John Loengard
American/New York, New York
Loengard originated the *Day in the Life* concept when he produced *One Day in the Life of America* as a *Life* magazine special report in 1974. A staff photographer for *Life* in the 1960s, Loengard went on to become the first picture editor of *People*. Instrumental in the revival of *Life* in 1978, he currently serves as the magazine's picture editor.

Saudi Arabia   1976

Gerd Ludwig
German/Hamburg, West Germany
A founding member of the Visum photo agency in Hamburg, Ludwig is a regular contributor to *GEO, Life, Zeit Magazin, Stern, Fortune* and other magazines. He is a member of Deutsche Gesellschaft für Fotografie (the German Photographic Society) and the Art Directors' Club of Germany.

Crombie McNeill
Canadian/Ottawa, Ontario
Chief photographer for the Ottawa *Journal* from 1964 to 1968, McNeill has been freelancing since 1969. His work has appeared in *Time, Newsweek, Life, National Geographic, Stern, Maclean's, Reader's Digest, Quest, Vogue* and *Skin Diver*.

Portugal   1972

Jay Maisel
American/New York, New York
Maisel's work appears regularly in magazines, advertisements and corporate publications. His color prints are included in numerous corporate and private collections. He received the Outstanding Achievement in Photography Award from the American Society of Magazine Photographers in 1978 and the Newhouse Citation from Syracuse University in 1979.

Ottawa   1948

Malak
Canadian/Ottawa, Ontario
Awarded the Gold Medal for Excellence by the National Film Board, Malak is the official photographer for the Netherlands Flower-Bulb Institute. He has had many exhibitions in Canada and the U.S., and for a number of years Canada's Department of External Affairs has featured his prints of Canada in a travelling exhibit.

Peter Martin
Canadian/Edmonton, Alberta
As a teenager, Martin was the official photographer for the Miss Teen and Miss Canada pageants. He joined *The Edmonton Sun* at the age of twenty-three and won the 1980 National Newspaper Award for Feature Photography. He has done fashion shoots in places like Tahiti, Hawaii, Hong Kong, Bangkok and Australia.

Harry Mattison
American/New York, New York
Mattison began his career as a photojournalist in 1978 covering the Nicaraguan revolution for Associated Press. He has extensively covered events in El Salvador. As a member of the Gamma Liaison picture agency, his work has appeared in *Time, The New York Times* and many major European magazines.

Stephanie Maze
American/Washington, D.C.
Born in New York and raised in Germany, Maze spent six years as a staff photographer for the San Francisco *Chronicle*. She covered the Montreal, Moscow and Los Angeles Olympic Games for the Associated Press and is now a freelance photographer who works primarily for *National Geographic*.

Dilip Mehta
Indian/Toronto, Ontario
Mehta is a former art director with several Canadian publications and television stations. He has produced four books on India and has contributed a wide variety of stories and photographs to international magazines including *GEO, Time, Bunte, Paris-Match* and the *Sunday Times* (London). He is associated with Contact Press Images.

Rudi Meisel
German/Hamburg, West Germany
Meisel is a founding member of Visum, one of West Germany's top photo agencies. Since 1975 his work has appeared in *Der Spiegel, Stern* and *GEO*. His assignments in East Germany were published as a book. His work has won numerous national and international awards.

Maddy Miller
American/New York, New York
Currently assistant photo editor at *People* magazine, Miller has worked for many major publications, beginning with freelance assignments for *Look* in 1970.

Robin Moyer
American/New York, New York
Moyer's coverage of the conflict in Lebanon was recognized with two prestigious awards in 1983: the Press Photo of the Year Award in the World Press Competition and the Robert Capa Gold Medal citation from the Overseas Press Club of America. Represented by the Black Star photo agency, his work appears regularly in *Time*.

Beirut   1983

Jim Nachtwey
American/New York, New York
A self-taught photographer, Nachtwey has covered world conflict from Ireland to Central America in the past four years. In 1983 he won two prestigious awards: Magazine Photographer of the Year from the National Press Photographers Association and the Robert Capa Gold Medal Award given by *Life* magazine and the Overseas Press Club.

A Day in the Life of Hawaii   1983

Matthew Naythons
American/San Francisco, California
A working photojournalist and physician, Naythons has spent most of his career alternating photo coverage of world events with emergency room duty in San Francisco. In 1979, he founded an emergency medical team to care for Cambodian and Thai refugees. His photographic work appears regularly in major magazines.

Roland Neveu
French/New York, New York
Neveu specializes in covering "hard news" stories for *Time, People* and *Fortune* and has been published in major magazines

around the world. He has worked extensively in Beirut, Afghanistan and Central America. He is associated with Gamma Liaison.

Kazuyoshi Nomachi
Japanese/Tokyo, Japan
Nomachi began freelancing in 1971 and since then has made several trips to North Africa and the Sinai resulting in the books, *Sahara* and *Sinai* published in five languages. He has also published books on the Nile and a second book on the Sahara which won Japan's Ken Domon Prize.

Al Normandin
Canadian/New York, New York
Originally from Vancouver, Normandin is a multi-media artist who works primarily as a color still photographer.

A Day in the Life of Australia   1981

Michael O'Brien
American/New York, New York
A native of Memphis, Tennessee, O'Brien began his career at the Miami *News* where his work was recognized with two R.F.K. journalism awards for outstanding coverage of the disadvantaged. His work now appears frequently in *Life, GEO* and other magazines.

Freeman Patterson
Canadian/Saint John, New Brunswick
A leading environmental photographer, Patterson has produced four books and has taught photography in Canada, the United States and southern Africa. He has won numerous awards for his work, including the National Film Board Gold Medal. He was awarded a Doctor of Letters Degree for Photography from the University of New Brunswick.

Colin Price
Canadian/Vancouver, B.C.
Winner of three Canadian Press Picture of the Month awards, Price was born in Vancouver and has worked in Edmonton, Montreal, Ottawa and Toronto.

Eli Reed
American/New York, New York
Reed is a veteran of the Middletown (N.Y.) *Record* and *The Detroit News*. For the San Francisco *Chronicle*, he has covered urban poverty and the conflicts in Central America and Lebanon. In 1982, he was granted the prestigious Nieman Fellowship at Harvard University. Reed is working on a book about the condition of blacks in North America twenty years after the civil rights movement.

Alon Reininger
Israeli/New York, New York
Upheavals in Nicaragua and El Salvador, developments in Honduras, the AIDS epidemic, the development of the Cruise and Pershing II missiles and cocaine smuggling in Florida are among Reininger's stories for the world's leading magazines. He is a founding member of Contact Press Images.

Science Digest   1984

Roger Ressmeyer
American/San Francisco, California
A 1975 graduate of Yale, Ressmeyer is a San Francisco based freelancer whose work has appeared in *Time, People, Fortune, Newsweek, Life* and *Science Digest*, among others. His specialties include portraiture, fashion, space and high technology. He founded the Starlight Photo Agency.

Afghanistan   1983

Reza
Iranian/Paris, France
A resident of France since 1981, Reza has covered the events in Iran after the revolution, the Iran-Iraq war and the American hostage crisis, as well as events in Afghanistan, Libya and the Middle East. He was awarded the World Press Photo News Feature Prize in 1984. His work may be seen regularly in *Time*.

Ken Sakamoto
American/Honolulu, Hawaii
Sakamoto has photographed the Royal Family at Windsor Castle and walrus hunts in the Arctic. His work has appeared in several Canadian newspapers, in *Time, Newsweek, Life* and *Sports Illustrated,* and in magazines in Europe, South America and Japan. He is currently a staff photographer for the Honolulu *Star-Bulletin* and is represented by the Black Star photo agency.

Bunte magazine   1984

Debra Streuber Schulke
American/Miami, Florida
Schulke's assignments have ranged from space shots to ancient religious sites in Hawaii to Christo's "Surrounded Islands." Her photos have appeared in *Newsweek, Bunte, Stern, Science Digest* and other international magazines. She has received many fellowships and awards and is associated with Black Star.

Mike Shayegani
Iranian/Los Angeles, California
Shayegani came to the U.S. from Iran in 1969 and attended Drexel University. After borrowing his father's camera at the age of fourteen, he developed an interest in photography and, several years later, moved to Los Angeles to begin freelancing. From 1979 to 1983, he worked as an assistant to glamor photographer Douglas Kirkland.

Bill Simpkins
Canadian/Calgary, Alberta
Simpkins worked for *The Calgary Herald* for fourteen years and is now employed in the Petro-Canada public affairs department. Simpkins' work has appeared in several magazines. He has published a book on Alberta and has won a Canadian Press award.

Tom Skudra
Canadian/Toronto, Ontario
Since 1967, Skudra has been working for a variety of clients in Canada and abroad including the Canadian government, *Maclean's, Quest, The Globe and Mail* and Labatt's Breweries. He has won several grants and awards and has exhibited his work across Canada.

South Korea   1981

Rick Smolan
American/New York, New York
Director of the *Day in the Life of Canada* project, Smolan is also responsible for *Day in the Life of Australia* (1981) and *Day in the Life of Hawaii* (1984). Prior to these extravaganzas, Smolan was

a full time photojournalist whose work appeared in major publications such as *Time* and *National Geographic*.

Barbados   1978

Boris Spremo
Canadian/Toronto, Ontario
Spremo began his newspaper career in Toronto in 1962 after emigrating to Canada in 1957 from his native Yugoslavia. He has won over 190 major national and international awards. He was the first Canadian to win a First Prize Gold Medal in the World Press Photo competition in The Hague in 1966. His work is published in many major magazines.

Andrew Stawicki
Canadian/Toronto, Ontario
After having worked as a staff photographer in Frankfurt for *Bild Zeitung* and in Warsaw for *Swiatowid*, Stawicki joined *The Toronto Star* in 1983. He has won prizes for his work in Poland and in Holland.

Greg Stott
Canadian/Toronto, Ontario
Originally a writer who took up photography to supplement his articles, Stott has become a photographer whose work is featured in many magazines. He conducts photo workshops and considers himself a Renaissance photographer who is "prepared to shoot any subject that is visually interesting."

Vince Streano
American/Los Angeles, California
Streano was a staff photographer with the *Los Angeles Times* from 1968 to 1973. Since then, he has been a freelance photojournalist for magazines such as *Smithsonian, National Geographic, GEO, Sports Illustrated, Forbes, Time* and *People*.

Peking   1973

Audrey Topping
American/New York, New York
A specialist on China, Topping has also worked in Vietnam, Cambodia, Central Asia, the U.S.S.R. and the Middle East. She has been published in major magazines including *National Geographic, Life, Horizon, Science Digest* and *The New York Times*, and has written four books on China and one on Tibet. Topping has worked on several television documentaries.

Dick Wallace
Canadian/Calgary, Alberta
A founding member of the Ontario News Photographers Association, Wallace served as its president from 1980 to 1981 and was named Photographer of the Year in 1980. He worked for *The London* (Ontario) *Free Press* for twenty-five years and for the past three years has been photo editor of *The Calgary Herald*. His over forty awards include the Michener Award for Meritorious Public Service in 1975.

Alex Webb
American/New York, New York
Webb's major studies include teenagers, Southern Evangelism, the Mississippi Delta, Southern Prisons, Haiti, Jamaica, the Mexican Border, Grenada, the Ivory Coast, Uganda and Washington, D.C. He has worked extensively for *The New York Times* and *GEO* and is a member of the Magnum Photo Agency.

Jim Wiley
Canadian/Toronto, Ontario
Winner of both Photographer of the Year and Picture of the Year in 1982 from the Ontario News Photographers Association, Wiley has worked with three major Canadian newspapers, the *Winnipeg Tribune*, the *Winnipeg Free Press* and *The Toronto Star*. His work has also appeared in *Maclean's, Quest* and *CFL Illustrated*.

Staff Members

The Book Project

Produced and Directed by
Rick Smolan and David Cohen

Project Co-Director
Douglas Kirkland

Director of Photography
Jack Corn

**Associate Director
of Photography**
Pauline Johnson

Logistics Co-ordinator
Bill Peabody

Production Co-ordinator
Jennifer Erwitt

**Public Relations
Co-ordinator**
Patti Richards

Office Manager
June White

Translator
Janet Heisey

Briefing Co-ordinator
John Durniak

Film Traffic Co-ordinator
Renata Haarhoff
Time, Inc.

**Film Processing
Co-ordinator**
Liz Detwiler
New York Filmworks

**Accommodations
Co-ordinators**
Hans Gerhardt
David Hamilton
The Sheraton Centre (Toronto)

Project Logo Design
Andrea Smith

**Administrative and
Production Assistants**
Wendy Brennan
Vivian Chapman
Bill DeKay
Rosalie Favell
Victor Fisher
Susan Kivi
Kai Sanburn
Pat Tagiolini
Rick Upton

Legal Advisors
F. Richard Pappas
*Paul, Weiss, Rifkind,
Wharton & Garrison*
Jory Kesten, W. Jack Millar
and John DeSipio
Blake, Cassels & Graydon

Business Advisors
Jeffery Epstein
First Boston Corporation
Bill Simpkins
Petro-Canada

Picture Editors
Brigitte Barkley
GEO (W. Germany)
Jocelyn Benzakin
JB Pictures
Elisabeth Biondi
GEO (U.S.A.)
Christiane Breustedt
Stern
Mark Bussell
The New York Times
G. Woodfin Camp
Woodfin Camp & Associates
Bob Carroll
United Press Canada
Jack Corn
Chicago Tribune
Ethan Hoffman
Archive Pictures
Kent Kobersteen
National Geographic
Eliane Laffont
Sygma Photos
Marijke Leupen
Maclean's
Steve Pigeon
Masterfile

Editing Facilities
Joy & Marty Solomon

Art Director
Leslie Smolan
Gottschalk + Ash Int'l.

Designer
Melissa Duffner
Gottschalk + Ash Int'l.

Design Assistants
Ann Harakawa
Brian Sisco
Gottschalk + Ash Int'l.

Captions
Audrey Topping
Rita D. Jacobs

Research Assistants
Susan Brownell
Evan Levine

Consulting Editor
J. Curtis Sanburn
Life

Collins Publishers
Nick Harris
President
Margaret Paull
Managing Editor
Frances McFadyen
Senior Editor
Michael Worek
Project Editor
Jenny Falconer
Production Co-ordinator
Peter Strachan
Sales Director
Sharron Budd
Publicity Manager
Eric Warot
Translator, French edition

Toppan Printing Co., Ltd.
Tetsuro Minami
Project General Manager
Shinichi Sugiura
Project Manager
Yuji Utsumi
Project Assistant Manager

The Documentary

Executive Producers
Rick Smolan and David Cohen

Co-ordinating Director
Sandy Smolan

Directors
Guy Borremans
Holly Dale
Jennifer Hodge
Adamee Mathewsie
Peter Raymont
Bill Roxborough
Ginger Turek

Videographers
Frank Beacham
Claude Gariepy
Brian Hebb
Martin Jarause
Al McPherson
Paul Mitchnik
Hernand Morris
John Phillips
Mark Rublee
John Sparks

Production Co-ordinators
Kai Sanburn
Ginger Turek

Conference
on Photojournalism

Co-ordinators
Bill Peabody
A Day in the Life of Canada
Lisa Matheson
Toronto Camera
Craig Thompson
NETSPEC

Agents

Canada
Steve Pigeon
Chris Moseley
Mike Fisher
Masterfile, Stock Photo Library
2 Carlton Street, #617
Toronto, M5B 1J3
Phone (416) 977-7267
In Vancouver (604) 734-2723

France
Annie Boulat, Cosmos
56 Boulevard de la Tour
   Maubourg
75007 Paris
Phone 705 4429, Telex 203085

Germany
Marita Kankowski, Focus
Schlueterstrasse 6
2000 Hamburg 13
Phone 44 3769, Telex 2164242

Hong Kong
The Stock House
310 Yue Yuet Lai Bldg
43-55 Wyndham Street
Hong Kong
Phone 5 220486 or 5 224073
Telex 78018

Italy
Grazia Neri
Via Parini, 9
20121 Milano
Tel 650832 or 650381
Telex 312575

Japan
Bob Kirschenbaum
Pacific Press
CPO 2051, Tokyo
Phone 264 3821, Telex 26206

United Kingdom
Terry Le Goubin
Colorific Photo Library
Gilray House, Gloucester
   Terrace, London W2
Phone (01) 723 5031 or 402 9595

United States
Woodfin Camp & Associates
415 Madison Avenue
New York, NY 10017
Phone (212) 750 1020
Telex 428788

Advisors, Contributors and Consultants

Michael Algar
Michèle Allard
John Allen
Fred Alts
Ian & Barbara Anderson
Ken & Libby Anderson
Barb Anonson
Bill Ardell
Derek Arnould
Steve Aronoff
Stewart Ash
The Ashini family
Suzanne Aziz
The Joseph Aziz family
Dale Ballard
Darlene Barker
Sheila Batt
Marianne Beamish
John ____ck
Jeannie Becker
Graham Bell
Brenda Bellair
Pam Bendalt
Richard Benfield
Liane Benoît
Len Berger
Gussie Bergerman
Rick Bertrand
Paule Berubé
Angela Bianchi
Linda Bierlmeier
Marie Binder
Don Blackwood
Roland Blanchard
Del Borer
André Bouchard
Odette Bouchard
Tan_ Bova
Cel_ Bowden
Pat Breckenridge
Doug Briggs
Bob Brock
Barb Bromley
Joyce Brookbank
Morry Brown
Gail Bryanton
Judy Bunbury & family
Maureen Bundgaard
Bob Burns
Eric Cable
Chief George Cakeway
John Calder
Bernard Campbell
Margaret Campbell
Dennis Cannon
D.A. Carp
William Carradine
Pat Carrington
Debra Caruso
The Caouette family
Christopher Cauly
Sandra Chabot
Ian Chapman
Stephen & Ruth Chappell
Zena Cherry
Josh Chiu
Judy Ann Christensen

Murray Church
George Ciauciones
Ron Clark
Pierre Cochard
Glenn Cochrane
Daniel Cohen
Gail Cohen
Hannah Cohen
Norman Cohen
Rose Cohen
Dan Colussy
Larry Condon
D. Conn
Bill Connor
Bob Cooper
Cathy Cooper
Lily Corewyn
Richard Cox
George Craig
Ted Croffield
W.H. Crone
Wally Crouter
Dr. & Mrs. Cruickshank
Jill Cunningham
Sandra Cunningham
Rod Currie
Dennis Curtis
Bill Dagget
Darryl Dahmer
Peter Dalglish
Don & Betty Dallyn
Julie Dalton
Don Dana
Val Daniels
Jeff Dave
Robyn Davidson
Hector Deault
Penny Demmingo
Mike Derblich
John Donald
Joan Donaldson
Sheila Donnelly
Al Downs
Arnold Drapkin
The Driskell family
Paul Drombolis
Mike Dukelow
The Dunn family
John Dye
Anne Eadie
Annie Edmonson
Mayor Art Eggleton
Christian Endemann
Mickey Endo
Arthur Erickson
Ellen Erwitt
Elliott Erwitt
Glen Etchegary
Gus Etchegary
Michael Evans
Hazel Farley
Jim Fetterly
Gordon Fisher
Gail Fisher-Taylor
Jack Fleischmann
Robert & Francis Flood
Evan Flude

Serge Forest
Albert Fortier
Michel Fournier
Don Foxgood
Barbara Fraser
Malcolm Fraser
Sig Front
Lynn Fruchter
Wallace Fulton
Jacques Gagnon
Roch Gagnon
Clodine Galipeau
Bernadette Gallez
Frank Gardiner
Ed Garton
Hans Gerhardt
Jane Ginsberg
Monique Giroux
Pam Glass
Elwood Glover
Paul Godfrey
Penny Gordon
Patrick Gossage
Marsha Graham
Maxine & Paul Graham
Tom Green
Woody Green
Ken Gregory
Sheldon Gross
Dale Gunn
Captain Brad Hall
David Hamilton
Michael Harris
Stu & Helen Hart
Maurice Harvey
Pattinson Hayton, Jr.
Larry & Ann Heisey
Kai Herbranson
Don Hill
Jeff Hill
Russ Holden
Russell Holder
Gary Hubbard & family
Dick Huisman
Christopher Hume
Martin Ingolls
Mark Ingrebrigtson
Edward Israel
Vern Iuppa
Peter Jackson
Henri Jamet
Peter Jansons
Jeff Jenkins
Beatrice Johnson
Major Eleanor Johnson
Dena Johnstone
Tom Jones
Margaret Kearny
Bob Keir
Nick Kendall
Betty Kennedy
Don Kerr
Jory Kesten
Meeka Kilabuk
David Killins
Mr. & Mrs. Morley Kirkland
Maureen Kitts

Chris Korwin-Kuczynski
Sgt. Dave Kowal
Len Kowalewich
Alvin Kumlin
Tony Kutney
Ana Lagowski
Fred Laing
Beth Langforth
Linda l'Aventure
Michel Lebas
Bill Lee
Diane LeGaurd
Bruce Legge
Larry Levin
Martin Levin
Brent Liddle
Ken Lieberman
Ray Lord
Greg Lowe
Don Lyons
Bob MacAdorey
Ron MacInnes
Terry MacLelland
Mary Majka
Al Mandell
Leslie Manning
Sylvia Manning
Dianne Marcino
Steve Markey
Mike Marshall
Art Matt
Gordon Matthews
Lucienne Matthews
Richard Matthews
Mike Mayzel
Adrienne McClellan
Stan McClellan
John McClelland
Gary McDermott
Mr. & Mrs. Leo McGraw
Barbara McLeod
Doug McLeod
Amanda McNamarra
George Meadows
Mona Mededward
Mac & Elaine Mercer
Mrs. D. Milliken
Tony Mina
Ida Mintz
Phillip Moffitt
John Monroe
Wendy Moore
Adam Morrison
R.C. Morrison
Dick & Barbara Morse
Chris Moseley
Uwe Mummenhoff
Barry Myers
Stan Myers
Knowlton Nash
Helen Jane Newman
Rick Nicholas
Lucy Nicholson
Chuck Novak
Dan O'Neil
Dan O'Shea
Mr. Ogilvy

Erik Olesen
Gunter Ott
The Bill Pardy family
Judy Parkin
Dave & Sue Patterson
Lorraine Patterson
Gabe Perle
Liz Perle
Stephanie Perry
Charlotte Pescenye
David Peterson
Jeff Peyton
Frank Pielak
Wayne Piercy
Roger Pike
Warick Pike
Elizabeth Pisani
Roger Pisani
Robert Pledge
Josette Poidevin
Joe Portogallo
Colin Price
Valerie Pringle
Patricia Pye
Paul Quassa
Kathy Quealy
Pat & Ivor Rage
Peter Ragmont
Shirley & Norman Ramsay
Tom Rektis
The Ted Ritchie family
Dr. Peter Roberts
Janine Robichaud
Bill Robinson
Patti Robson
Tom Rose
Duncan Ross
Ed Roworth
Barbara Royds
Mark Rublee
The Russell family
Sheila Ryan
Tom Ryder
André Sauvageau
The Rt. Hon. Jeanne Sauvé
Barbara Sawetzki
Bob Schiffer
Ellen Schoenfeld
Dave Schultz
Leonard Sclafani
Mel Scott
Dr. Robert Scott
Gary Sebastian
Nikki Seligman
Sandra Severn
Ann Jennings Shackelford
Bob Sharp
Leanne Sharp
Hugh Siegal
Bill Simpkins
Bob Siroka
The Hon. John Sloan
Andrea Smith
The Hon. David Smith
Gail Smith
Randy Smith
Rod Smith

Gloria Smolan
Marvin Smolan
Rob Snare
Don Snyder
Edwarda Souza
Ian Stark
Mark Starowicz
Bonny Stazer
Ernest Stefanson
Gene Stevens
Helen Stiles
Carol Stillar
Jim Stockton
Sheldon Suga
Eltie Sutherland
Nancy Suttles
Joan Sutton
Dave Swan
Mitsuhiro Tada
Mr. Tailleur
Mosesee Tautuasuk
Frank Taylor
Stuart Taylor
Shirley Teasdale
Françoise Théberge
Cal Thomas
Norm & Beatrice Thomas
Craig Thompson
Capt. Ian Thompson
Tom Thomson
Mike Thorpe
Walter Tilden
John Trafford
Sylvia Train
Jean-Claude Tremblay
Jack Troake
Father Guy Trudel
Della Van Heyst
Valerie Verlak
Claire Verreault
Susan Walker
Cecile Ward
Melanie Ward
Dave Warren
Calvin Waterman
Judy Webb
Don West
Cherie Westmoreland
Mike Wheeler
Margaret White & family
George Wiesman
Dr. M. E. Wilson
Paul Wilson
Dave Winer
Peter Winer
Jim Winter
Sharon Winter
Greg Wjunenko
Nancy Wolff
Peter Workman
Simon Worrin
Bob Wright
John Wright
Nina Kaiden Wright
Allan Young
David Young
Rita Zekas

Sponsors

Underwriter
Petro-Canada

Exhibit Underwriter
American Express Canada Inc.

Subsidizer
Canon Cameras

Major Sponsors
The Sheraton Centre
CP Air
Kodak Canada, Inc.
New York Filmworks
Lowe Alpine Systems
Daymen Photo Marketing

Major Contributors
Apple Computer
Coopers & Lybrand
Tilden Rent-a-car

Contributors

Advance Planning
Agropure
Alberta Tourism
 and Small Business
Alpine Adventures
Annapolis Valley Affiliated
 Boards of Trade
Arts & Communications
 Counsellors
Australian High Commission
Bache Securities
Banff Chamber of Commerce
Banff School of Fine Arts
Best Western Motor Hotel,
 Niagara Falls
Bio Engineering Institute,
 University of New Brunswick
Boise Cascade Canada Ltd.
Canada Post
Canadian Armed Forces
Canadian Forces Base,
 Petawawa, Ontario
Canadian Union of Public
 Service Employees
Cape Breton Tourist
 Association
CFRB Radio
CFTR Radio
Chez Pierre's Cabaret

CITY TV, Toronto
CJCA Flying Tiger
CKEY Radio
CKO Radio
Club 32
Compass Rose
Contact Press Images
Convention Inn South
Cory Potash Mines
Council of Metropolitan
 Toronto
Cowan, Liebovitz & Laitman
Department of External Affairs
Dvorkian Meat Packers
Eastern Breeders, Inc.
Eastman Kodak
Edmonton City
 Fire Department
Edmonton City
 Police Department
Edmonton Space Sciences
 Centre
Edmonton Symphony Orchestra
Eighty-eight Ferry Restaurant
Elmwood School
Environment Canada
Equitable Life Assurance Co.
Estevan Chamber of Commerce
Fathom Five Underwater Park
First Air
First Insurance
Fishery Products Ltd.
Fort Garry Hotel
Fort McMurray Chamber
 of Commerce
Gaspésie Tourist Association
General Videotex Corporation
Gottschalk + Ash, Toronto
Grace Maternity Hospital
Grenfell Regional Health
 Service Hospital
Headwaters Fishing Camp
Highlands Community School
Horizon Type, Inc.
Hotel Royal
Inco Ltd.
International Telephone
 & Telegraph
Inuit Broadcasting Corporation

Iuppa McCarten Associates
J.E. Henning School
Jack's Hunting Lodge
Jean-Jacques Olier School
Klondike Visitors Association
Kluane National Park
Kootenay Boundary Visitors
 Association
Labatt's Breweries
Labrador Airways
Lake of the Woods Regional
 Information Centre
Laura Secord Ltd.
Life magazine
Living Videotex Corporation
Louis Tussaud's Waxworks
Manalta Coal Mines
Manitoba Department
 of Tourism
Maple Sugar Country Bureau
 of Tourism
Mendelssohn Commercial Ltd.
Metropolitan Toronto
 Clerk's Department
Metropolitan Toronto Police
Metropolitan Toronto Separate
 School Board
Mitel Corporation
Montreal Expos
Morse Century Farm
National Ballet School
National Geographic Society
National Research Council
National Rubber Co.
New Brunswick Department
 of Tourism
New Brunswick Mining
 & Smelting Corp.
New Dimensions in Travel
Nichele Photos
Nisku Inn, Edmonton
Northwest Territories,
 Department of Tourism
Office of the Chairman
 of Metropolitan Toronto
Office of the Mayor of Toronto
Office of the Prime Minister
Office of the Speaker of
 the House of Commons
Okanagan Tourist Association
Ontario Crippled Children's
 Society

Ontario Ministry of
 Correctional Services
Ontario Ministry of
 Natural Resources
Ontario Ministry of Tourism
 & Recreation
Ontario Ministry of Transpor-
 tation & Communications
Pacific Rim Airlines
Palette Productions
Panarctic Oils Ltd.
Peace Bridge
Peter Pond Hotel
Peyton Lodge
Prince Rupert Chamber
 of Commerce
Provincial Forest Fire
 Control Centres
Quebec Tourism Office
Queen Street Camera Exchange
Rage's Farm
Rat Portage Indian Reserve
Regional Municipality
 of Sudbury
Rocky Mountain Visitors
 Association
Royal Alexandra Hospital
Royal Canadian Mint
Royal Canadian Mounted Police
Royal Canadian Mounted
 Police Training Academy
Rudolf Hennig School
Rutherford Audio-Visual
Ryerson Polytechnical Institute
Saskatchewan Telecommuni-
 cations
Smokey Kettle Maple
 Company Ltd.
South Shore Tourism Association
Southam, Inc.
Southwestern Alberta Tourist
 Association
Southwestern British Columbia
 Tourist Association
Southwestern Ontario
 Travel Association
St. John's Chamber
 of Commerce
Stanford University
Stewart Color

Stryker Weiner Associates
Sudbury Aviation Ltd.
Syncrude
T-shirt Wearhouse
Technigraphic
Ted Bates Associates
The Copy Shop
The Robb Report
The Snowbirds
The White House
Tilden Rent-a-car
Time, Incorporated
Time magazine
Toppan Printing
Toronto Camera
Toronto City Clerk's
 Department
Toronto Eaton Centre
Toronto Sesquicentennial Board
Toronto Stock Exchange
Tourism B.C.
Tourism Canada
Town of Tillsonburg
Travel Alberta
Triple Five Corporation
United Airlines
Universal Speakers
University of British Columbia
 Health Services Centre
 Hospital
Vancouver Public Aquarium
Vancouver Whitecaps
Vanderhoof Chamber
 of Commerce
Wardair
Warkworth Medium Security
 Prison
Western Development Museum
Western Fair Raceway
Western Inn
Western Rodeo Boot
Wilderness Tours
Young Men's Christian
 Association of Canada
Yousuf Karsh Studio

Colin Price

All *A Day in the Life of Canada* photographers used Kodak Film and Paper.

A Day in the Life of Canada is much more than the book you are holding in your hands. It is a project which captured the imagination of thousands of Canadians and involved people from around the globe—people who made the tremendous leap of faith necessary for this project to take place.

We are grateful to the 100 photographers who flew to Toronto from all over Canada and the world to apply their rare and prodigious skills with devotion, to the thousands who photographed alongside the professionals, to the business community of Canada, which contributed so generously, and to the more than 2,000 individuals who participated in the final production. This book is a tribute to each of you and to Canada.